All of the author's proceeds from this book go to ScholarMatch, a nonprofit organization that increases college access for low-income students of exceptional promise.

For more information, visit www.scholarmatch.org.

AT HOME ON THE RANGE

At
HOME
on the
RANGE

A cookbook presented by
Elizabeth Gilbert

By her great-grandmother
Margaret Yardley Potter

McSWEENEY'S BOOKS

SAN FRANCISCO

www.mcsweeneys.net

Cover by Gold Collective and McSweeney's.
Interior illustrations by Shannon May.
Endpapers recreated from the first edition.

McSweeney's and colophon are registered trademarks of McSweeney's,
a privately held company with wildly fluctuating resources.

ISBN: 978-1-936365-89-0

Contents

Foreword

by ELIZABETH GILBERT

This cookbook has been around my family a lot longer than I have. *At Home on the Range* was first published in 1947, back when my father—now a grey-bearded man in flannel shirts—was a towheaded toddler in droopy pants. The book was dedicated to my Aunt Nancy, whom the author described as a five-year-old child already in possession of the "two prime requisites of a good cook: a hearty appetite and a sense of humor." (Nancy is still in possession of both those fine qualities, I am happy to say, but she is now a grandmother.) The copy of the cookbook that I inherited belonged to my own grandmother, our beloved and long-gone Nini, whose penciled notes ("Never apologize for your cooking!") are still in the margins. The book was written by her mother—my great-grandmother—who was a cooking columnist for the *Wilmington Star*, and who died of alcoholism long before I was born. Her name was Margaret Yardley Potter, but everyone in my family called her Gima, and until this year, I had never read a word of her writing.

Of course, I'd seen the book on family bookshelves, and had certainly heard the name Gima mentioned with love and longing, but I'd never actually opened the volume. I'm not sure why. Maybe I was busy. Maybe I was prejudiced, didn't expect much from the writing: the original jacket photo shows a kindly white-haired woman with set curls and glasses, and maybe I thought the work would reflect that photo—dated and ordinary, JELL-O and SPAM. Or maybe I am just a fool, willing to travel the world in pursuit of magic and exoticism while ignoring more intimate marvels right here at home.

The author photo from the first edition.

All I can say is that I finally picked up Gima's cookbook this spring at the age of forty-one, when I found it at the bottom of a box, which I was finally unpacking because I was finally settling into the house where I hope and pray to finally stay put. I cracked it open and read it in one rapt sitting. No, that's not entirely true: I wasn't really sitting, or at least not for long. After the first few pages, I jumped up and dashed through the house to find my husband, so I could read parts of it to him: *Listen to this! The humor! The insight! The sophistication!* Then I followed him around the kitchen while he was making our dinner (lamb shanks), and I continued reading aloud as we ate. Then the two of us sat for hours over the dirty dishes, finishing a bottle of wine and taking turns reading the book to each other by candlelight.

By the end of the night there were three of us sitting at that table.

Gima had come to join us, and she was wonderful, and I was in love.

What you have to understand about my great-grandmother, first and foremost, was that she was born rich. Not stinkin' rich—not Park Avenue rich, or Newport rich—but late nineteenth-century Main Line Philadelphia rich, which was still pretty darn rich. I tend to forget that we ever had that strain of wealth and refinement in our family (probably because both were long spent by the time I arrived) but—decidedly unlike her descendants—Gima grew up with sailboats and lawn tennis, white linens and Irish servants, social registers and debutante balls.

The young Margaret Yardley was not a beauty. That would've been her little sister, Elizabeth (for whom I was named.) A family visitor, introduced to both girls when they were in their teens, let his eyes rest on my great-grandmother and said, "Well, you must be the one who cooks." Well, yes, she was the one who cooked—and she also happened to be the charming and popular one. With such nice credentials, she probably could've married just about anyone. For reasons lost to history, she chose to marry my great-grandfather Sheldon Potter—a charismatic Philadelphia lawyer full of brains and temper and narcissism, who was witty but lacerating, sentimental but unfaithful, who'd passed the bar at age nineteen and could quote Herodotus in Greek, but who never developed a taste for work. (As one disapproving relative later diagnosed him, "He was too heavy for light work, and too light for heavy work.")

Sheldon Potter did, however, develop a taste for fine living and for serious overspending. As a result, Gima slid deeper and deeper into reduced circumstances with every year of her life. As she relays (uncomplainingly!) in the first pages of her cookbook, over the course of her marriage she was "shuttled financially and physically between a twelve-room house in the suburbs, a four-room shack in the country, numerous summer cottages, and a small city apartment." She passed the lean years of World War II on "an isolated and heatless farm on Maryland's Eastern Shore," which was probably the furthest imaginable cry from her classy Edwardian upbringing.

Listen, she made the best of it. For one thing, her financial troubles were not *entirely* Sheldon's fault: Gima was quite the spendthrift herself, and she faced life with a Jazz Age sensibility that can best be summed up in one gleeful, reckless, consequence-be-damned word: *Enjoy!* Moreover, she had an instinct for bohemian living—maybe even a preference for it, and that instinct informs the winningly informal tone of *At Home on the Range*. While she admits, for instance, that "there is no substitute for either good food or a comfortable bed," she submits that pretty much everything else in the material world *can* be substituted, or improvised, or gone without, or cobbled together from junk-store treasures. Books can be borrowed, wildflowers can be picked from roadside ditches, barrels can be transformed into perfectly good little tables, orange crates make for excellent chairs, cheap onions can replace expensive shallots without anyone's tasting the difference, and there's no need whatsoever to be ashamed of a kitchen that resembles "an old-fashioned tin peddler's cart." All your guests really need from you, Gima assures us, is your warm welcome, plenty of good food, and a steady supply of ice for cocktails. Provide that, she promises, and "a world of friends will beat a path to your door."

So she *did* provide, and so a world of friends *did* beat a path to her door, but it should not be inferred that her life was necessarily easy just because her houseguests adored her. Married to a man whom my father describes as "impossible," constantly in debt (sometimes slipping out of foreclosed homes just ahead of the sheriff's arrival), struggling with the alcoholism that would periodically land her in psychiatric clinics and grim hospital wards, my creative but constrained great-grandmother was not the first or the last woman in the history of female hardship to take refuge in food.

Gima in her garden.

Or rather, I should say, she took refuge both in food and in *writing*, because the voice that emerges on these pages is a literary delight as well as a culinary one. Gima doesn't just list her recipes here, she *tells* her recipes, with wit and self-confidence that make her sound like a cross between Dorothy Parker and M.F.K. Fisher. (Don't overthink orange marmalade, she assures us in one typically bright passage: "Constant stirring and average intelligence is really all that's necessary.") Gima was also a food sensualist, a quality all too often missing in American cookbooks from that era. Not only does she carefully explain how to bake a perfect loaf of bread, but just as the loaf is coming out of the oven she adds, "And if you can resist cutting off a big warm piece and spreading it thickly with butter, you're not the girl I think."

But what strikes me most, reading Gima's cookbook, is that she was so far ahead of her time. *At Home on the Range* was published right between the end of World War II and the onset of 1950's—right at that unfortunate moment in American culinary history when our country was embarking on its regrettable love affair with convenient and processed foods, with canned goods and electrical appliances, with powdered mashed potato mixes and easy-breezy marshmallow salads. Gima was having none of it. Instead, she encouraged her readers to *explore*, to *dare*, and most of all, *to do it by hand*. What follows is only a partial list of the recipes she was cheerleading while the rest of the country tucked into Birds Eye frozen peas and quick-heat TV dinners:

BRAINS WITH BLACK BUTTER

CHICKEN LIVERS FOR SIX

BEEF AND KIDNEY PIE

TONGUE

EELS (which she reports having first discovered during wartime meat shortages, and which, she believes, are so delicious they must be "devoured in a silence almost devout")

TRIPE (which must be hand-scrubbed "like a bath towel" before cooking—a process that is, she swears, "more fun than it sounds")

COCKSCOMBS WITH WINE (collected in buckets from puzzled local poultry farmers)

BOILED ROCK FISH (hand caught, and then hand-sewn into one of your husband's old undershirts with a half-dozen other fresh ingredients)

WILD GRAPE JELLY ("picking the fruit yourself beneath a blue fall sky is half the pleasure")

ANTIPASTO WITH FRESH SARDINES

SCRAPPLE

CALVES' HEAD CHEESE (a "grand hot-weather snack!")

MUSSELS (which she bemoans as being "an insufficiently known delight" on this side of the Atlantic)

And on it goes, making me wonder *who* was she writing this *for?*

These days, I have about twenty friends who would happily scrub raw tripe like a bath towel, or eat cockscombs straight off a freshly scalped rooster, but this is *now*, this is 2012, when unshrinking foodie exploration is all the rage. Gima, on the other hand, was writing at the dawn of the baby boom, when it *wasn't*. This is perhaps why her book only came out in one edition. Maybe people weren't yet ready for her appetites. Like mussels in mid-twentieth-century America, maybe she herself was doomed to be an insufficiently known delight.

But in both cases (with bivalves and great-grandmothers alike) better late than never, right? And Margaret Yardley Potter is certainly worth getting to sufficiently know now. Almost a generation before Julia Child, my great-grandmother was not merely a terrific cook, but also a dogged food reporter, an intrepid food explorer, and a curious food historian. She wasn't afraid to wander back into the kitchen of some ritzy hotel or swanky transatlantic ocean liner to bribe a sauce recipe out of a flattered French chef. But she also managed—between contractions—to extract a fantastic pickle recipe from the friendly nurse who helped deliver her first child.

And speaking of motherhood, when Gima was hugely pregnant with my grandmother (this would be 1918), she was eating her way through an Italian neighborhood in Philadelphia one day when she discovered "a warm, brownish red pastry" called "Italian tomato pie, or pizza," and thereupon convinced "the ancient proprietress" of the shop to teach her how to make it. How many other respectable—and knocked up!—ladies from good Main Line Philadelphia families were wandering around immigrant neighborhoods in 1918, not only eating pizza with the denizens, *but learning how to make it at home?* She also learned how to make fricasseed rabbit from a Pennsylvania Dutch farm woman, baked beans from a handyman's wife in a Maine fishing camp, and quick tea cookies from a handwritten cookbook she'd bought at a rural yard sale. (The elderly farmer who sold it to her claimed the book had been "his grandmom's mom's"—which means, as of today, that recipe is nearly two hundred years old. You can find it on page 121, and it's lovely.)

Gima plucking a goose.

It's impossible to read all this lively writing and culinary exploration without wondering, *My god, what might she have become?* In a different time or place, what might Gima have made of all her curiosity and passion and talent? And that is the sad question that leads me to the story about my great-grandmother and Paris. Or, rather, the story that is *almost* about Paris.

The tale goes like this: In the mid-1930s, Margaret Yardley Potter walked out on her impossible husband Sheldon. She'd had enough of him. There was talk of a divorce. I don't know how close they came to actually filing papers, but she definitely moved out and lived on her own for a while. (I suspect she may be referring to that episode when she writes in her cookbook that every woman should know how to mix her own cocktails, in case her husband is indisposed, or in case the hostess in question "lives alone and likes it.") In any case, Gima left her husband and formulated a plan—or maybe we should call it a dream. She would take her teenage daughter and relocate to Paris, where they would live with her Uncle Charlie, who was an established portrait painter over there. (Her college-age son would stay back in the States and finish his schooling.)

According to family lore, there was something scandalous in Uncle Charlie's past that had probably sent him over to Paris in the first place. There is talk that he might have had an affair with a married woman, which had driven him out of polite Philadelphia society. Whatever his transgressions, my great-grandmother cherished him. Uncle Charlie, in fact, makes several appearances in this cookbook, most notably when Gima relates visiting him in France as a young woman and eating a "thrilling lunch" in his lofty studio—"disappointingly empty of beautiful undraped women"—where she learned, by the end of the afternoon, how to mix a perfect vinaigrette. She also, quite obviously, learned from Uncle Charlie how to love France, and she always wanted to return there. You need only read two pages of her book to recognize that she *belonged* in France: it's where her sensibilities' standards could have been met, where her talents could have been recognized, and where her *confrères* could have been found. Imagine the people she might have encountered there! Imagine the food she might have eaten! The books she might have written!

Well, she *almost* moved there, anyhow. I still have the passport photo of her and my young grandmother, seated together in silk dresses and perfect hairdos, looking regal and sophisticated and absolutely ready to hop on the next ocean liner… but they never went. Instead, Gima returned to her impossible husband, with her passport and daughter in tow. She remained with Sheldon until she died in her early sixties. He, on the other hand, remarried and lived quite happily until the age of ninety-nine and three quarters—drinking and eating and smoking and reading with rather impressive gusto right till the end. I was sixteen years old when he died, so I knew my great-grandfather well. He awed and delighted me, and gave me challenging reading assignments whenever I came to visit. I have always believed that his inspired bookishness was one of the reasons I became a writer. I didn't realize until reading *At Home on the Range* that Gima may also have been a contributing factor to my vocation—that there may be such a thing as a Family Voice, and that I may have been lucky enough to have inherited some of mine from Margaret Yardley Potter.

Ultimately, I don't know why Gima went back to her husband instead of pursuing her dream of Paris. Nobody knows. Maybe she didn't have the cash or the courage to go. Or maybe she just missed him. I can tell you this much: every single reference she makes to that man in her cookbook is affectionate—but *credibly* affectionate, by which I mean that she writes of her husband fondly, but not without undertones of undisguised domestic tension. It sounds like a real marriage, in other words. A good example is her description of their kitchen blackboard, which, she reports, is frequently chalked over with teasing spousal messages like "Where did you put the bottle opener, you bum?" Cute, yes—though also telling, on many levels.

Margaret and Madeleine Potter.

Whatever her reasons, she went back home. Something in me wishes she hadn't, even though it would've changed our family history so dramatically that some of us—me, for instance—would not exist. It's a silly wish. It's always a naive instinct to want to rewrite history, anyhow, and there's probably something *particularly* naive about my belief that Gima could've had a happier and healthier life as a divorced woman in Europe. The fact is, she was an alcoholic, and nobody's alcoholism ever got cured by simply changing locations. (Certainly nobody's alcoholism ever got cured by moving to *Paris in the 1930s*.) But still. You can imagine how she would have been in her element there. And if there is a heaven for cooks—and my great-grandmother insists in these very pages that "surely there is one"—then I would like to believe that Gima is in that heaven, and that it bears an uncanny resemblance to the country of France.

Gima is still dearly missed within our family.

She died in 1955, but my relatives still get emotional when they talk about her. She was, it is consistently proclaimed, the most wonderful woman you ever knew. The funniest, the brightest, the most marvelous, the most loving, the center of every party. She could make a Christmas celebration pop like nothing you ever saw. My dad's happiest memories of childhood were Christmases spent with Gima, when they would make edible ornaments by baking a loop of string straight into the cookies—the recipe is in this book!—and then they would hang the cookies directly on the tree… and then the family dogs would knock over the tree to get at the cookie-ornaments, but nobody seemed to care. Indeed, "nobody seemed to care" is how a lot of stories about my great-grandmother's legendary parties end: she didn't mind the furniture getting thrown around the room a little bit, it appears, as along as everyone was having fun.

She was certainly a warm and generous woman, as evidenced by her core tenets regarding hospitality, which include "Try not to forget your friends' birthdays," or "Be lavish with the coffee," or "Try not to let those unexpected guests feel that you are embarrassed by their sudden appearance—half the time, they are a little embarrassed themselves." I found myself quite moved by the chapter "Open Your Mouth and Say 'Ah-ha,'" where Gima lists recipes that are good for sick friends who are stuck in the hospital. (These range from cinnamon buns or simple deviled eggs to—on the happy night before the patient's release—a smuggled-in bottle of champagne and a celebratory tin of caviar.) Ask yourself if you have *ever* seen another gourmet cookbook in which recipes are included for hospitalized friends. And it goes beyond mere food! If the patient is a child, my great-grandmother further suggests, be sure to bring him a little goldfish in a glass bowl, or one of those tiny turtles you can buy at any pet store; this will go far in easing a sick child's boredom and loneliness. When I think of all the time Gima herself spent alone in hospitals and institutions, these pages feel only more poignant. I just hope somebody in her life was bringing *her* cinnamon buns and baby turtles.

So her loss is still felt keenly by all my relatives. But she outlived herself in some ways, if that makes sense. What I mean is—some parts of herself have outlasted other parts of herself, and can still be found, scattered among us.

Her kitchen has outlived her: My cousin Alexa has its contents—down to the least serviceable utensil—in her house in Baltimore.

Her recipes have outlived her: I grew up eating Gima's chutney and Gima's pickles, prepared by my Midwestern mother, who never met the woman, but who fell in love with the cookbook.

Her name has outlived her: my Uncle Nick named his daughter Margaret, in honor of his irreplaceable grandmother.

Her humor has outlived her: for instance, whenever we play cards in our family, we still say, "Help yourself to the stewed fruit," which was the catchphrase Gima delivered every time she got dealt a lousy hand.

And her passions have outlived her, still manifesting themselves quite firmly, four generations later, through the pursuits and aspirations of her female descendants. Among her six great-granddaughters, three of us write for a living, one of us runs a restaurant, one of us is a hostess worthy of any recipe in this book, two of us are wizards at cards, two of us are trained historians and three of us found a way to live overseas. All of us love a good party. Gima also has two preteen great-*great*-granddaughters, who are not only charismatic and literary, but in whom the "prime requisites" of—yes!—"hearty appetite and sense of humor" have come down the pike utterly intact.

What I'm saying is, if you are influential enough and beloved enough, it turns out you can stick around for quite a while after you die.

When, in preparation for writing this essay, I asked my family for memories of Gima, my uncle Nick sent this email: "Christmas 1969. You are zero years old. Dad and Mom and me and Nancy your parents and you two kids are all squeezed into that little dining room on Moore Avenue, and there are candles, and John and I are back from the war, and everything's just wonderful. Then your father says, 'This would all be perfect if only Gima were here.' And Mom sighed and said, 'Well, that's that.'"

Well, that *is* that.

We all wish she could've stuck around a lot longer, but what can you do? As Gima herself might've said, "Help yourself to the stewed fruit." It is what it is, folks. She stayed as long as she could. But what she left behind was something quite remarkable. My hope, with this new edition of her cookbook, is that in our generation she will finally find her readers, her peers, her admirers, the culinary *confrères* she always deserved.

On Gima's behalf, then, it is my great pleasure to make this introduction. *Enjoy.*

At Home on the Range

For my granddaughter Nancy Root Gilbert who at the age of
five years already has the two prime requisites of a good cook:
A hearty appetite and a sense of humor

Introduction

by Margaret Yardley Potter

This is a book for simple cooking and entertaining, which in my case was learned the hard way, for I started housekeeping in the all-too-glorious early 1920s when servants and food were plentiful and cheap. Dinners, even for four, were always formal; while the best gold-edged place plates, white-capped maids and a fish course were expected when more than six sat down to partake of, though not always to enjoy, dinner.

My own formal entertaining had a short life and ended within the first three years of my married career. By then a small son and a baby daughter had appeared to complicate matters, and nurses who would pinch-hit as waitresses were becoming increasingly hard to find. Nevertheless I persevered with the formality my mother had preached, doing my best to live up to her beautiful standards of living. Until, finally, there arrived the fatal day when I prepared the dinner that was to honor a very important and dignified guest, little knowing it was to be my last affair of the sort.

It began with the usual telephone discussions, and the promise of mother's butler for the occasion. With her help this menu was finally evolved—we thought it a simple one, too:

Cocktails   Caviar

Oysters on the half-shell with cocktail sauce

Clear green turtle soup

Broiled shad roe with sauce tartare in lemon baskets

New potatoes with parsley butter

Small brown bread sandwiches

Sliced cucumbers in French dressing

Celery   Radishes   Olives

Broiled chicken   New peas

Hot rolls

Fresh pineapple salad—served in the whole fruit

Cream cheese   Hot toasted water biscuits   Bar-le-Duc

The whole was finished off by one of those wonderful three-decker meringues for which Philadelphia caterers are still famous—followed of course by coffee and brandy in the living room, and afterwards three sedate tables of bridge.

Came the day of the dinner and also the food I had ordered; but, too, by noon came the news that the borrowed butler was on his half-yearly binge and totally unable to buttle, while that juvenile delinquent, my thoughtless baby daughter, showed signs of developing croup, and demanded much more than her share of nurse's attention. Undaunted, I rolled up my sleeves and, side by side with cook, went to work. She made tartare sauce while I cut lemon baskets, the edges of which looked as though they had been bitten instead of pinked. I sliced cucumbers and brown bread; she prepared chickens, shad roe and shelled endless peas. (No Mr. Birds Eye and his lovely ready-to-cook frozen kind in those unenlightened days!) I gave up all thought of the salad and soup courses; and thanked heaven for the dependable caterer and his towering meringue which must, I felt, give my amputated dinner a final finishing touch of formality and splendor. By five in the afternoon everything was done—the lace-covered table sparkled with glass and silver, the best dishes stood ready in rows, and cook and I retired, she to snatch a short rest before her further work began, I to beautify what remained of me.

My pretty young sister, the second guest of honor, arrived at the house, bag and baggage, about six o'clock, listened with heartfelt sympathy to my tale of woe, swore she would be in there pitching as soon as she was dressed, then retired to her room, plugged in her electric vibrator and *phft!* every light in the house went out and, what's more, stayed out all evening. One result of which was that it took an extra half-hour to round up two of our guests who, arriving on time and seeing our darkened windows, had gone home without ringing the bell, sure that they had mistaken the date; while the candles in the kitchen only seemed to intensify the gloomy depths from which cook's voice spoke of an approaching nervous headache. Nurse, still radiating a slight croup-kettle odor of eucalyptus, announced dinner after the hurried cocktails, and my own nerves only relaxed when the remains of the juicy chicken that followed plump salt oysters and perfectly broiled shad roe, were removed from the table. Alas, things were going too well! Just as dessert was due a wail from the nursery caused the "waitress" to disappear like Cinderella at midnight, with a whisper to me that cook would surely be able to carry on for the concluding course. Resigned but confident, I pushed the kitchen buzzer, waited, *pushed* the buzzer, waited, pushed the buzzer, then tottered through the pantry door. There in the kitchen sat cook, head in hands amidst unstacked dishes and guttering candles, gazing out of tear-filled eyes at a partially unwrapped meringue. The threatened headache was a grim reality and the poor creature could barely get upstairs. Bravely trying to keep some remnant of what I still felt was the necessary formality, I was just about to bring the meringue to the table when the guest of honor appeared in the kitchen and, with a heartening pat on my back, bore the icy pyramid to the dining-room sideboard where, amidst cheers, he announced himself as the new butler and proceeded to serve the dessert and jovially press second and third helpings with all the confidence of a stage "Jeems." Coffee and brandy, still dignified by silver tray and cut glass decanter, were escorted into the living room by my husband, but by that time all formality had vanished and my guests continued what they maintained was their most enjoyable evening in years by shooting craps on the floor with the light of every remaining candle. When the electric company's lineman arrived at eleven-thirty to fix a blown main fuse he was invited to try a few "rolls" before he finished the meringue, and he departed for his next call considerably richer. Our important guest really relished his kitchen supper of beer and selfmade onion sandwiches and when later he joined a game of softball in the hall, batting one of the baby's worsted toys with a rubber-tipped plumber's assistant, his dignity and my failure as a formal hostess were both completely forgotten, and I realized that elaborate entertaining with inadequate help was neither convincing nor worth the nerve-shattering effort.

Since then I have been shuttled financially and physically between a twelve-room house in the suburbs, a four-room shack in the country, numerous summer cottages and a small city apartment. An isolated and heatless farm on Maryland's Eastern Shore was my home during the war years. In all of these abodes I have found that providing a really heartfelt welcome and simple and plentiful food gives any hostess an advantage over the famous man who built the better mousetrap. A world of friends will beat a path to your door.

Weekend Guests Without a Weakened Hostess

Along winter of grippe and flu had taken its toll of the children's health; the doctor, with complete disregard for our balance, recommended a summer near the ocean for us and after much searching we found, in our favorite New Jersey resort, a five-room native house that we could afford. It had no dining room and no bathtub, neither of much consequence we felt, but the primitive two-burner oilstove that stood in a corner of the big kitchen looked anything but promising, its later behavior lived up to its earlier threats. The living-room sofa unfolded into a not-too-uncomfortable double bed and this proved such a temptation to my always hospitable husband that it was a rare Friday that I returned from a late afternoon on the beach without finding him and two weekend guests getting into their bathing suits.

Sea air makes for hunger and I soon discovered that, unless I cooked beforehand for this onslaught, I spent aproned Saturdays and Sundays in solitary confinement, juggling pots and pans over the smelly stove. Then and there began my system of planning ahead that stands me in good stead till this day.

On the back porch was a big old-fashioned ice chest and the latter part of each week saw it so crammed that it was difficult to shut the lid. Thursday night, white sauce, boiled potatoes, cooked rice, mayonnaise, French dressing, shredded cabbage and shelled peas struggled for room on its shelves with a stewed cut-up chicken, peeled tomatoes and washed lettuce, while ground meat or, when we felt really flush, a big beefsteak, was ordered for Saturday's delivery. Friday I deprived my helpless offspring of their morn-

ing trip to the beach, and before I baked their midday fish and potatoes in the big tin oven that covered the whole top of the stove, I had ready a layer cake, a pie and rice or bread pudding to go in at the same time. After that I relaxed, freed from heavy cooking until Monday.

Our weekend menu varied very little but gave me lots of time to enjoy our guests.

Friday night we had easily prepared hot boiled lobsters or fried soft-shell crabs—both cheap in those happy days—hashed brown potatoes and cole slaw, with cake and fresh fruit to accompany our final cup of coffee.

Breakfasts, I admit, were unimaginative. My guests got cold cereal and eggs and bacon with their tomato juice and coffee, and liked it or else!

Saturday mornings we left the children with a sitter, wrote out directions for their dinner and simple supper, packed a picnic basket with tomato and leftover bacon sandwiches and made a few more of potted meat and pickle. We added a thermos jug of coffee and the pie, and were off for the day in a cheap hired motorboat, so decrepit a vessel that the time of our return—if at all—was always doubtful. We were more than ready for dinner when we did get home and dinner was ready for us, or nearly so. The cold potatoes were covered with white sauce and put on to heat in the double boiler while our green vegetable cooked on the second burner. In the meantime, the cut-up chicken was mixed with mayonnaise and celery, heaped on lettuce and garnished with tomatoes. With a little more time, I made a curry of fowl, heated up the rice, and had big side dishes of sliced tomatoes and onion rings covered with French dressing. Fruit again, with a sharp cheese or more cake finished this meal.

As a rule, our guests left early Sunday evening so we had dinner late in the afternoon to allow for a long morning on the beach, though I'm sure you can guess who it was that took the children home for their early meal and nap! It was always pointed out that I had all the empty week ahead to bask so I didn't much mind missing all the strand's Sunday gaiety and gossip. *Not Much!*

When my sunburned trio finally appeared, preceded usually by an aura of gin and attended by a wistful group of pals who had been collected at various cocktail parties, I fed the hungry horde pan-broiled meat cakes or beefsteak, more cole slaw or tomatoes. For vegetables I had boiled noodles and fresh corn, both of which could be done in the five or ten minutes the cooked meat stood off the stove, covered, to bring out every drop of its flavorsome juice. I put the meat in the center of a big hot platter, wreathed it with noodles, and poured over them the lovely pan gravy to which I'd added a little butter and water and a few drops of Worcestershire sauce.

For dessert we had the rice pudding and what I'd been able to save of the cake. If enough of my pie had weathered the weekend I sometimes cut that into pieces and put a scoop of drugstore ice cream on each one.

The menu I have suggested would be even simpler to prepare on an up-to-date stove and welcomes substitution. Cold cooked meat loaf for the higher priced chicken, a thick slice of ham to take the place of the beefsteak, and a toothsome lamb stew ready for a few minutes reheating, would make for a labor-saving weekend. Do as much cooking ahead as you can, have three or four possible combinations of the food in your icebox tucked away in your brain or, better still, written down, and you'll not only be able to laugh on Monday at hostesses worn out by three days of ceaseless cooking but can speed your departing guests without dropping exhausted on the front steps as their car goes out of sight.

ADDITIONAL WEEKEND MENUS

These have, of necessity, a certain amount of repetition and the lists for preparation look long, but a great many of the activities take very little time or can proceed simultaneously with others. Use covered dishes which will stack in the refrigerator.

MENU NUMBER I

Friday Dinner

Broiled fish with lemon butter. . . . . page 97

Hashed brown potatoes . . . . page 160

Cucumbers stuffed with spinach . . . . page 89

Fruit compote . . . . page 176

Cake. . . . . page 110

Saturday or Sunday Lunch

Cream of pea soup with croutons . . . . page 42

Tossed salad with shredded ham,

Roquefort cheese dressing. . . . . page 101

Hot gingerbread (use a mix)

Saturday Dinner

Veal cutlet with tomatoes and eggplant . . . . . . page 55

Baked potatoes

Cole slaw . . . . page 102

Trifle . . . . page 111

Special Late-Sunday Breakfast

    Fruit juice

    Cold cereal

    Kidney stew .page 190

    Waffles . . . . .page 194

    Coffee

Sunday Dinner

    Meat cakes with broiled tomatoes . . . . page 52

    Potatoes au gratin . . . . .page 160

    Peas

    Drop biscuits .page 144

    Pie . . . . .page 117

PREPARATION

Asterisked items* should be put in refrigerator, covered. Karated items^ may be leftovers.

Wednesday night

    Soak peas for soup.

Thursday

    Cook and dice potatoes*

    Cook and chop spinach*^

    Slice onions*

    Cook string beans*^

    Make three-layer cake, ice two layers

    Make piecrust, roll to fit plate*

    Make fruit compote*

    Boil kidneys for stew*

Friday

    Make boiled custard, pour over extra layer of cake for trifle*

    Make French dressing*

    Wash lettuce*

Wash tomatoes for Sunday*

Make kidney stew*

Parboil cucumbers, stuff with spinach*

Shred ham*

Make cole slaw*

Prepare green vegetable for Sunday, if not quick frozen*

Scrub baking potatoes

Bread and brown eggplant*^

Bread and brown veal cutlet*^

Cook tomatoes 15 minutes*^

WHEN READY TO EAT

You have now made practically all of your necessary preparation; sit down, relax, and await the arrival of your guests. Something remains to be done, but not too much:

Friday Dinner

Broil fish, brown stuffed cucumbers in same oven at same time; hash brown the potatoes.

Saturday Lunch

Thin the pea soup with milk and heat; toast and cut croutons; mix salad; make gingerbread.

Saturday Dinner

Brown onions and place in casserole with veal cutlet, eggplant, etc., and bake; bake potatoes in same oven at same time.

Sunday Breakfast

Reheat kidney stew; bake waffles at table.

Sunday Dinner

Cover potatoes with white sauce and bake; broil meat cakes and tomatoes in same oven, also bake drop biscuits; cook green vegetable; warm pie.

MENU NUMBER 2 (LESS EXPENSIVE)

Friday Dinner

Saturday Lunch

Cheese

Saturday Dinner

Cooked fruit

Sunday Dinner

Small new potatoes boiled in their jackets

Green salad

PREPARATION

Thursday

Make Cherry Ring*

Boil potatoes*

Make cole slaw*

Slice cucumbers, put in serving bowl, cover with French dressing*

Make white sauce*

Make clam chowder*

Friday

Hard boil eggs, stuff some for Saturday lunch.

Boil and flake fish, and put fish and hard-boiled eggs in greased casserole*

Make stuffing for tomatoes*

Boil macaroni, put in greased casserole with cheese*

Cook fruit*

Mix and bake cake*

Make lamb stew*

Make Crème Brulée, do not glaze*

Wash lettuce*

Wash tomatoes*

WHEN READY TO EAT

Friday Dinner

Cover fish with bread crumbs and white sauce and bake; fry potatoes; boil, drain and butter asparagus.

Saturday Lunch

Reheat clam chowder; make potato salad.

Saturday Dinner

Cover macaroni with white sauce, bake; brown sausage cakes, finish in oven; stuff tomatoes, bake in same oven; glacé Crème Brulée with sugar, at same time, and return to icebox.

Sunday Dinner

Reheat lamb stew; boil potatoes; boil peas and put on top of stew before serving.

MENU NUMBER 3

Friday Dinner

Saturday Lunch

Warmed French bread

Cold cuts

Tomato salad

Saturday Dinner

Baked slice of ham with candied

Green vegetable

Corn bread (use mix)

Fresh fruit

Sunday Dinner

Rice

PREPARATION

Thursday

Boil and dice potatoes*

Cook asparagus*

Make vinaigrette dressing*

Make French dressing*

Make dough for cinnamon bun*

Parboil peppers*

Friday

Parboil sweet potatoes*

Prepare green vegetable for Saturday*

Bake cinnamon bun*

Wash lettuce*

Make cole slaw*

Boil chicken and cut in pieces*

Make creole sauce*

Boil and drain rice*

Cook small amount of vegetables for Sunday salad or plan leftovers*

Make and bake pie

Prepare flour and shortening for pudding*

Prepare crab meat, put in peppers, arrange in greased dish*

Make onion soup (use chicken stock)*

WHEN READY TO EAT

Friday Dinner

Bake crab meat; add milk and egg to pudding mix and pour over cherries, bake in same oven with crab meat; fry potatoes; cover asparagus with vinaigrette dressing.

Saturday Lunch

Reheat onion soup; make salad.

Saturday Dinner

Surround ham slice with sweet potatoes and apple rings and bake; boil green vegetable; reheat cinnamon bun.

Sunday Dinner

Reheat chicken in creole sauce; reheat rice; prepare salad; warm pie.

A Soupçon on Soups

O ur narrow city house rose four high stories above its basement kitchen and the only mechanical means of communication between the floors were metal speaking tubes which emitted tuneful whistles but not much else. Fortunately, the inside rooms opened on an unsanitary but handy air well, and the whole family, even my dignified mother, found this a much more convenient way of conversing with Jane, our faithful Irish cook. The bang of a raised window always brought her questioning, "Ma'am?" wafting upwards, and the voice that descended generally demanded, "Have we enough soup? There's going to be company." Jane must always have hoped for a more unusual message, for her bored, "Yes'm" reechoed glumly as she retreated to her kitchen cave.

Jane guarded her secrets well and just how she produced the never-failing flow of soup was somewhat of a mystery. But since I was to her that paradox, "a young lady who likes to cook," she broke her rule before I was married and gave me a hint by showing me how to make her wonderful VEGETABLE SOUP. Start it with 3 pounds of beef a half of which should be bone. "Soup meat" is a safe thing to ask for at a reliable butcher's, or a good combination is 1½ pounds of any cut of lean beef and a shinbone. Cut the meat into inch pieces and brown half of it quickly in a little of its fat in the pot you will use for the soup. Add the rest of the meat and the bones, cover with 4 quarts of cold water, and let it stand for ½ hour. Cover and simmer for 1 hour and add ¼ cup each of chopped carrots, onion, and celery (also turnips if you have them), 1 sprig of parsley, a pinch of thyme, and a bit of bay leaf. Continue simmering, covered, for at least 2 hours longer—all day if you wish—and 1 hour before removing from the fire add 1 tablespoon of salt. Strain and add the pieces of meat and let it cool, covered. There you have the "soup stock" which no well-run kitchen ever used to be without. Nowadays the contents of the red-and-white cans have taken its place and are almost as good, except in this hearty dish. Leave 2 tablespoons of fat on the stock to add to its flavor and remove the rest. Bring the stock to a boil and add 1 can of tomatoes or 1 pint of ripe peeled ones, 1 teaspoon of chopped parsley, and 2 tablespoons of barley or rice. Follow these with 1 teaspoon of sugar, ½ cup each of peeled onions and carrots, the same amount of celery or its leaves, and ¼ cup of cabbage or turnips, all cut into small pieces. Taste for seasoning, add extra salt if needed, and simmer 2 or 3 hours before serving with crackers, biscuits, or toast. Accompany it with a salad for a delicious and nourishing lunch or light supper.

This is just the basic recipe, and, as you get expert, it can be kept going for days. Into the pot goes more new, or any leftover, meat and vegetables and the water they were cooked in. Peas, okra, lima or string beans, corn, asparagus, noodles, spaghetti, macaroni, and potatoes, each and all are good additions. Don't use too high a proportion of any one thing. Cut the vegetables into pieces. Go carefully with the strongly flavored broccoli, cabbage, and turnips. Keep the ratio of liquid to vegetables 3 or 4 to 1, and if things get too thick add tomato juice, canned consommé, or water.

A very habit-forming dish, and we had it so often one seaside summer that the family call for the afternoon and evening meals became "Soup's on." Our untrained maid took it up, and after we went home in the fall it was some time before she could remember, even before company, to return to the conventional, "Dinner is served."

More quickly prepared and a good imitation of the meatier homemade brand is VEGETABLE SOUP NUMBER 2. It serves four or six. Melt 1 tablespoon of butter and in it cook over medium heat ½ cup each of coarsely chopped onion, carrots, and celery or its leaves. Let them get soft but not brown. Add 4 cut-up tomatoes, peeled or canned, and 2 cans of condensed bouillon or consommé which has been diluted with an equal amount of plain water or that in which vegetables have been cooked, and ¼ teaspoon of sugar. Simmer for at least ½ hour, and when in a real hurry put the vegetables through a grinder or food mill before cooking. Season with salt if needed.

VEGETABLE SOUP NUMBER 3, for four or six. Melt 1 tablespoon of butter and soften in it ½ cup each of finely chopped celery leaves, green onion tops, carrots and watercress, and ¼ cup of the outside leaves of lettuce chopped as finely. Add 1 cup of tomato juice and 1 can of condensed consommé diluted with twice its amount of water or cooked vegetable juice. Simmer for ½ hour or longer.

Clear hot soup is the best beginning for a filling dinner or lunch and, although Jane would think you lazy, canned consommé or bouillon answers exceedingly well if its tinned taste is removed. All you have to do to banish tinniness is to dilute the soup with an equal quantity of tomato juice, add a slice of lemon or 1 teaspoon of whipped or sour cream to each serving and a sprinkle of parsley, and you might have stewed and strained over a hot kettle for hours for all the difference in flavor. This is, of course, TOMATO BOUILLON or CONSOMMÉ as the case may be and a dash of curry powder and no cream puts À L'INDIENNE after its first name. Try diluting the condensed soup with only half its quantity of water, put 1 teaspoon of dry sherry in the bottom of each cup and float on a slice of lemon, 1 teaspoon of chopped hard-boiled egg and parsley. Just a good bouillon but no trace of the can. Add a few dice of ripe avocado pear and it's an IMITATION CLEAR GREEN TURTLE SOUP, and a fine one.

CLAM BISQUE and OYSTER BISQUE are made exactly alike. Add 2 or 3 chopped bivalves to 1 pint of their strained juice and bring to a boil. Make 1 pint of white sauce (page 94). Have it hot in a double boiler and mix in the steaming juice. That is all there is to it, except a warning not to boil the finished product. CLAM CONSOMMÉ is hot strained clam juice, with or without chopped clams, sometimes dressed with a float of whipped cream. CONSOMMÉ BELLEVUE is clear clam juice brought to a boil with an equal quantity of chicken broth and topped with whipped cream and a pinch of chopped chives. A delicious tangy soup to which the famous Philadelphia hotel is proud to give its name.

Dried split green peas are the foundation of three of the finest thick soups there are, and these directions will give you enough to try each one. Read the package carefully and if the peas are not labeled "quick cooking" soak 2 cups of them over night in 1 quart of water and drain. Cut a 2 inch cube of salt pork into dice, fry it until crisp and brown, and reserve. Cook ¼ cup each of chopped onion, carrots, and celery in the fat until soft. Add the soaked peas and 4 cups of water, 1 tablespoon of salt and ¼ teaspoon of black pepper. Simmer until the peas are tender and soft, keeping them covered with water. Force them through a sieve or food mill. The quick-cooking peas will take about ½ hour, the others from 3 to 4 hours, to cook. For OLD-FASHIONED PEA SOUP melt 1 tablespoon of bacon fat and add 1 tablespoon of flour. Cook over a medium heat for a few minutes and slowly add 4 cups of water and 1½ cups of the strained peas. Let come to a boil and serve topped with the crisp bits of pork. CREAM OF SPLIT PEAS is made by melting 1 tablespoon of butter over a medium heat, stirring in 1 tablespoon of flour and slowly adding 4 cups of thin cream or milk and 1 cup of strained peas. Pass toast croutons with this. PEA MULLIGATAWNY. Prepare butter and flour as above, slowly add 4 cups of tomato juice, 1 cup of strained peas, and ½ teaspoon of curry powder. More curry may be needed, depending upon brand used, but there should be just a suggestion of it in the finished soup. This is an almost undetectable imitation of a much more complicated and difficult soup.

In the spring and early summer, when fresh green peas are abundant, make PEA VICHYSSOISE for four or six. Boil 1 cup of peas in enough chicken broth to cover them—about 2 cups—until tender, and put through a sieve or food mill. Prepare butter and flour as above, slowly stir in 3 cups of thin cream or top milk and the sieved peas, and let come to a boil. Taste for salt and serve it in your best soup cups, each cup floating ½ teaspoon of finely chopped chives or green onion tops, for the perfect start of a luncheon. Thin warm Melba toast should go along.

BORSCH is vegetable soup with a Russian accent. For four or six, soften 1 cup of shredded cabbage and 1 tablespoon each of chopped onion and carrot in 2 tablespoons of butter. Add 1 cup of chopped canned beets, ½ cup of their juice, 1 tablespoon of vinegar, and 5 cups of beef stock with a few pieces of the cooked meat, or 3 cups of canned consommé or bouillon and 2 cups of water. Simmer for at least 1 hour. Season with salt if necessary and serve with a tablespoon of sour cream on each helping.

The traditional Christmas Eve dish in our house is FRENCH ONION SOUP. Melt 3 tablespoons of butter, add 1 tablespoon of finely chopped celery leaves, 1 tablespoon of grated carrot, and 3 cups of thinly sliced onions separated into rings. Cover and cook over a medium fire until the onions are very soft and yellow. Add 5 cups of stock or 3 cups of condensed bouillon and 2 cups of water and 1 tablespoon of grated Parmesan cheese. Let simmer 45 minutes, covered, and taste for salt. You will find this to be a more oniony soup than the usual kind but, as the cross old lady said when a stranger told her that her slip was showing, "I like it that way." Serve it to four or six on thick slices of toasted French bread and pass grated Parmesan or Romano cheese. Don't, if you can help it, use for this or for any other recipe calling for grated Parmesan, the grated pasteurized "Italian Type," whatever that means. It is the kind that comes sealed in shaker-top cans with all its real flavor killed. Almost any Italian grocery carries a variety of hard cheeses. There must be such a one somewhere near you and the proprietor will be glad to advise your selection and often grate it for you. Or take a quarter pound home and do your own grating. You'll have twice as much for half the money, and much better at that. I made a permanent friend of a dignified bank president by sending him every week during a long hospital convalescence a gaily decorated package containing a pint of onion soup, two pieces of toast, and an envelope of grated cheese. It was his favorite dish, but frowned on in his home; at last, he happily maintained, he could enjoy it unmolested. I can't believe that the soup is accepted sickroom diet but I do know that a steaming cup as a "morning after" pickup will restore one kind of invalid to full health in a miraculously short time.

CHESAPEAKE BOUILLABAISSE is the best fish soup in the world this side of Marseille. For four or six, heat ½ cup of olive oil—no substitutes here, please—and soften in it ¾ cup of chopped onions, 1 chopped garlic clove, 1 tablespoon of grated carrot, and 1 tablespoon of chopped celery leaves. Add a pinch of fresh dill, rosemary, and basil, if you have them. Add 4 skinned or canned tomatoes, 1 inch of lemon peel shredded, and simmer 15 minutes. Put the bones from 2½ pounds of filleted fish, and 2 fish heads, if possible, in a saucepan and lay the fish on top. Add 2 slices of onion, a small piece each of bay leaf and mace and 6 peppercorns. Cover with 3 cups of water and 1 cup of white wine. Add 1 teaspoon of salt and simmer until the fish is just tender. Remove it and reserve. Simmer the fish bones and heads at least 1 hour longer in the same liquid. Strain, add water if necessary to make 4 cups. Add it to the vegetables and let simmer, covered, 1 hour longer. Add ½ cup of canned mussels and ½ cup of shelled cooked shrimps, canned or fresh; cooked lobster or crab meat can go in this, too, in ½ cup quantities.

Add the cooked fish, bring to a quick boil, add extra salt if necessary, and serve each helping over a piece of toasted French bread. Any kind of fish, fresh or frozen, is good in this, but try to have at least two, or better, three varieties. If the fish are small, remove as many bones as possible after cooking and before adding to the cooked stock. Add a pinch of powdered saffron from the drugstore, if you want to go completely Thackeray. This recipe might make a French bouillabaisse enthusiast shudder—before he tasted it—but it is delicious and filling and after all there is no reason why we shouldn't be culinary trailblazers on this side of the ocean, too.

Hearty LENTIL SOUP seems to be an almost forgotten dish. Soak 1½ cups of lentils overnight and drain. Melt 1 tablespoon of butter, soften in it 2 tablespoons of chopped onion, 1 tablespoon of chopped carrot and 1 tablespoon of chopped celery leaves. Add the lentils, 8 cups of water, 2 teaspoons of salt, ¼ teaspoon of pepper, and a pinch of cayenne, and simmer until the lentils are very soft. Remove from the fire and break up the lentils a little, with a potato masher or heavy spoon. Melt 1 tablespoon of butter, add 1 tablespoon of flour, blend, and slowly add the lentils. Add 2 frankfurters cut in thin slices, simmer, covered, 15 minutes, and serve. On a cold blustery day, "when the wind goes 'who-oo,' " no goblins—or gremlins—will ever git you with a big bowl of this tucked under your belt.

Pot Roast à la Mode Sentimentale and Other Less Corny Meats

It doesn't seem such a long time since I stood at my window and watched a small blond boy off for his first day at kindergarten. The gilt buttons on his navy-blue reefer twinkled in the bright fall sun and he stopped at the crossing and looked carefully up and down as he'd been instructed before he made a dash across the street. Then a round hat with a proud "U.S. Navy" on the band was waved in my direction, a little voice came back, "I'm all right, Mom, don't you worry," and the momentous instant was for both of us over.

Almost overnight, as I look back on it, the lad was off to boarding school in his first long trousers. Then came college, and now he's married, and another little blond boy has the same name and is taking almost the same walk to the same kindergarten, and probably will be off to the same school and college too, before I know it. Right now the band should burst into "Dear Little Boy o' Mine," with undertones of "Mammy," but I must admit that most of my memories of those days have to do with getting name tags sewed on clothes and being sure he made the right train back to school. But the homecomings! For years they had an identical pattern. First, up went the flag, not so much from patriotism, I regret to say, as from the fact that his adoring but pretending-to-be jealous younger sister once announced in mock rage that "we did everything but put up the flag" when her brother came home. But always, a few days before the homecoming, in answer to plaintive letters that his first night's meal be this beloved dish, I started preparing pot roast.

Later, for four years, the boy was back in his original navy blue. He came with his wife and small son to spend his pre-embarkation leave with us before shoving off for Japan. We're not, you can easily gather, a sentimental family, but when he saw the Stars and Stripes proudly waving over the door, sniffed as he came in, gave me a look and said, "Pot Roast, Mom?" I think we both felt a little choky. He's back now, and the flag and the POT ROAST were ready for his permanent homecoming, and here's how that looked-forward-to dish is prepared.

First, I take a 4- or 5-pound piece of top-of-the-round beef and a pint or so of red wine, claret or Burgundy, domestic if necessary, but good. Never try to cook with poor wine. You wouldn't drink it, would you? Put the meat into a shallow bowl, pour the wine over, and add 2 sliced onions and 1 crushed garlic clove, ½ cup of finely chopped celery, a pinch of thyme, and a bit of bay leaf if you like the taste. We don't, but most people seem to. Let it soak for 24 hours at least, turning the meat every 8 hours or so. When you are ready to cook, drain the meat thoroughly, reserving the wine, and mop it as dry as possible. (I use a paper towel lightly). Dust the meat with flour. Now try out 4 ounces of suet or chopped salt pork in a deep kettle. Put in the beef and brown it thoroughly on all sides, pour in the wine marinade (first fishing out the bay leaves), add 4 peeled tomatoes, and let it just simmer, tightly covered, for 1 good long hour. Then add 2 peeled onions and 2 scraped whole carrots for each person you expect to serve. A few peeled turnips won't hurt, either. About a tablespoon of salt and a good big dash of pepper are indicated here. From now on it's simply a question of when the vegetables are done, but another hour of slow cooking seems about right. In the meantime have ready 2 packages of broad noodles that have been boiled in plenty of salted water. Drain them and keep them hot in a colander over boiling water.

Now comes the exciting moment. Put your roast on a large hot platter, thicken the gravy with ½ cup of sour cream while bringing the juice to a low boil. Add a little cornstarch or flour mixed with cold water, if not thick enough. Place the vegetables around the roast, then decorate the edge of the dish with great spoonfuls of the hot boiled noodles, each mound of which has a bit of butter nestling on its top. Serve the gravy separately.

A big bowl of salad for which the returned hero made the dressing, one of Mom's pies for dessert with a bit of cheese on the side, lots of coffee all through the meal, and there can be no better Welcome Home feast whether he's back from school or war.

ROAST LAMB needn't be the tasteless dish—hot or cold—that's found on most tables. A real leg of baby spring lamb well cooked, I grant you, can't be improved upon, but when you are a bit doubtful of the age and texture of your mutton, try it this way:

For 1 leg of lamb allow 2 cupfuls of finely chopped parsley mixed with 1 teaspoon of chopped chives or green onion tops. Now with a sharp thin knife (I use a small steak carver) cut 4 or 5 small slits in the meat, not too close together, and through to the bone. Pack each one as tightly as you can with the chopped greens. Cut a clove of garlic in slivers and insert them under the skin in odd spots, and skewer 3 or 4 lamb kidneys, with half their fat removed, underneath the roast. If the meat seems lean put a piece of kidney fat on top, too. Now rub the whole well with flour and salt and pepper, put it and a cup of red wine and water, half and half, in an uncovered baking pan, and let it cook in a moderate 350° oven at least ½ hour to the pound. Take a look at it every so often and baste it with the essence in the pan. When half done remove the piece of kidney fat, if you've used it, and surround the joint with 2 small whole peeled carrots, 2 peeled onions, and 2 peeled and parboiled white potatoes for each diner. Baste with more wine and water if the pan gets dry. When finished the vegetables should be just brown and the meat crisp outside and moist and juicy within. Add a little flour and water to the juice in the pan, let it boil up, and such a gravy you will have! I don't believe that you will find either currant or mint jelly necessary with this treat.

Now you will have leftover lamb, and what to do? That's easy. Try DEVILED MUTTON. Make a marinade in the proportion of 4 tablespoons of cooking oil, 4 tablespoons of sharp vinegar, 2 tablespoons of English mustard, and 1 teaspoon of Worcestershire sauce, and just cover thin slices of meat with this. Let it sit all night if you wish. Melt a little butter in a large iron frying pan, and when it sizzles put in your meat and brown on both sides. Add any leftover gravy, the marinade and enough water to cover; then thicken the sauce a little if necessary. Let it simmer ½ hour, serve on a bed of rice or hot broad noodles, and pass the chutney. And is it good! The raw mustard taste that you expect seems to vanish completely and the result is an indescribable flavor.

This recipe came from St. Lucia in the British West Indies, where the climate is hot and the meat fresh killed and stringy, so something has to be done about it. I ate it there at the lovely little Hotel St. Antoine whose proprietress wanted to know, of all things, how to make real Boston baked beans. So we traded recipes and both felt that we'd come out ahead.

SMOTHERED CHICKEN for six. Rich, expensive, and delicious. Broil 3 small tender chickens 5 minutes on each side in a hot oven. When well browned, cut in half. Melt ½ pound of butter in a large iron skillet, add 2 tablespoons of flour, 1 teaspoon of salt, and stir until well blended. Add 1 pint, or a little more, of cream, slowly, and cook until thickened. Put in the chickens, cover the skillet, and let everything simmer in a medium 350° oven for ½ hour or a little longer if you wish. This is a fine dinner dish to follow a hot or cold clear soup. Accompany it with crisp French fried potatoes and a tart salad.

CHICKEN CACCIATORE is made for six with 2 three-pound frying chickens cut up, dusted with flour, salt and pepper, and browned in ½ cup of olive oil. Fish out the chicken, put the pieces in a casserole, and add to the oil a chopped garlic clove, 1 cup of chopped onions, and an optional pinch of sweet basil and rosemary. When the onions are soft, pour in 1 can of tomatoes and 2 tablespoons of tomato paste. Let this simmer for 15 minutes. Pour over the chickens, cover tightly, and cook in a 350° oven for 45 minutes. Serve it with buttered boiled spaghetti, and pass the grated Romano or Parmesan cheese.

Sultry weather calls for old-fashioned PRESSED CHICKEN as my grandmother made it. One mouthful, and cool breezes blew. The age of the bird does not matter in this recipe. The older, tougher fellows take longer to cook but seem to give a better flavor. Cover 1 large cut-up stewing chicken with cold water, simmer for 1 hour, add 1 teaspoon of salt, and continue cooking until very tender. This may take 3 hours if your bird is a veteran. Strain, remove the skin and bones, and return them to the broth. Cut the meat into small pieces and pack in a greased mould. Boil the broth with the skin and bones until you have only 3 cups left. Then let it cool and skim off every bit of fat. Rewarm the broth, season with salt and pepper, and pour carefully over the meat. Chill until solid, overnight preferably. Turn from the mould onto lettuce, and surround with sliced hard-boiled eggs and quartered tomatoes.

COUNTRY STEWED CHICKEN for six. Cut a 5½ or 6-pound chicken into pieces. If it is a good big one, each leg, second joint and quarter of the breast will make a helping. Put in a kettle and add enough cold water just to cover it. Add 1 small chopped onion and 1 teaspoon each of chopped celery tops and parsley. Cover and simmer until done, adding salt before quite tender. Drain the chicken. Let the broth cool and skim off the fat. Melt 4 tablespoons of the fat and add slowly 3 tablespoons of flour. Stir in 3½ cups of the chicken broth and ½ cup of cream, cook until thickened, add the chicken, let it heat thoroughly, and serve surrounded by rice and small corn fritters (page 88).

CHICKEN LIVERS WITH RED WINE for six. Sauté 1 tablespoon of chopped onion or chives, 1 teaspoon of parsley, and ½ pound of sliced mushrooms, in 3 tablespoons of butter until the onions are soft. Add 1 pound of chicken livers dusted with 3 tablespoons of flour, 1 teaspoon of salt and a little pepper. Let cook 5 minutes. Add 1 cup of dry red wine and 2 cups of bouillon, consommé or chicken broth. Cook 10 minutes until thickened. Serve in a ring of 4 cups of cooked rice, and with fried eggplant. If there is any of this dinner left over, mix the rice and livers with 2 or 3 chopped peeled tomatoes, canned or fresh; add 1 chopped onion, 1 chopped garlic clove and 1 chopped green pepper that have been softened in a little butter, to the fried eggplant cut in cubes. Mix together and put in a small greased casserole, cover, and bake 1 hour in a 375° oven for a delicious and unusual luncheon dish.

HAMBURGERS mean to too many of us just overdone bits of pasty, greasy, flavorless meat, slapped between cold rolls at a wayside diner, but there is no reason why they shouldn't be delicious. Don't, I beg, buy already ground, unidentified "hamburg" from the meat counter. Get top or bottom of the round and have the butcher grind it just once, under your watchful eye. Failing this, run it through your own meat grinder, using the medium cutter, and following it with a small onion for each pound of meat. Mix it well with 4 tablespoons of chopped parsley and perhaps a few chopped celery leaves. Then gently, to give the juices plenty of room, form each pound into not more than 6 good-sized, not-too-thin cakes. Have your iron skillet very hot and just wipe the bottom with a bit of bacon, salt pork, or suet. Cook the cakes until they are a crisp brown outside and a tender pink within. Give them about 4, and certainly not more than 5 minutes on each side. Have half a freshly toasted roll for each meat cake ready on a warm plate, put on a hamburger, and keep them hot while you add 1 tablespoon of water for each serving to the juice that is left in the pan. Season each meat cake with salt and pepper, pour over a little of the gravy, and cover with its twin half of the toasted roll. For trimmings try green and red pepper rings fried in butter, or slices of onion treated the same way. Thick slices of broiled tomato, first dipped in crumbs, and topped with a dab of butter, go well under the meat, and mustard pickle and India relish are almost necessary accompaniments. For something different, surround each meat cake with a slice of bacon fastened with a toothpick or string before you cook them. Either plain or baconed, they are good with spaghetti or creole sauce, too.

MEAT LOAF is easy to make and can be a real party dish. Almost any combination of cooked or raw meat will do, and this is an excellent standard recipe for six or eight. Take 1 pound of lean beef, ½ pound of raw ham, with a little of the fat, ½ pound of raw veal, from the knuckle if you wish, and grind them together twice with 2 raw scraped carrots, 2 peeled onions, 1 stalk of celery and 2 large sprigs of parsley. Add 2 beaten eggs and ½ cup of bread crumbs, ¼ teaspoon of thyme, salt, pepper, ½ teaspoon of dry mustard and 1 teaspoon of Worcestershire sauce. Mix well and form into a loaf. Put in a greased baking pan and lay three slices of bacon on top. Pour over it 1 can of condensed tomato soup and bake in a 375° oven 1 hour. If the pan seems dry baste with a little water or red wine. Good, hot or cold! Like many other dishes its variations are endless. Instead of tomato soup, chop 2 fresh peeled tomatoes, or their equal in canned, with the meat and baste the loaf with red or white wine. A few chopped slices of Virginia ham or salt pork will change the flavor again, and if you are planning to serve it cold, a row of shelled hard-boiled eggs placed in the interior of the loaf before baking are not only ornamental when cut but make it go further.

IRISH SHEPHERD'S PIE is simply an old dish glamourized, and it's a wonderful way to use up any leftover combination of beef, veal, or lamb. For six people take 2 cups of ground cooked meat. If the measure isn't quite full make up the difference with bread crumbs, but not more than ½ cup. Add 1 chopped carrot and 2 tablespoons of chopped celery. Perhaps a few pieces of chopped leftover bacon. Brown ½ cup of chopped onion and ½ chopped green pepper in 3 tablespoons of fat, add 1 tablespoon of flour, and slowly stir in 1 cup of leftover gravy or canned consommé, and ½ cup of red wine, and let it boil up again. Put in the meat and simmer for 5 minutes while you stir. It shouldn't be too dry—you're making a juicy pie filling so if it doesn't seem quite moist enough, and especially if you have used crumbs for a "stretcher," you may need a little more liquid. Cut 3 green peppers in half, lengthways, remove the seeds and white ribs, parboil for 5 minutes, and drain. Butter a pie pan and line it with the peppers, skin side down and small ends toward the center, and spread the meat filling evenly over them. Behold, your "pie" in its "crust." For the "meringue" put 2½ cups of boiled white potatoes through the ricer, or mash them, and thoroughly beat into them ¾ of a cup of hot milk. Season highly with salt, black pepper, and a scrape of onion, heap them in peaks on the pie, and dribble 2 more tablespoons of milk over it before you slide it into the oven to bake at 375° for 30 minutes.

The same filling makes an excellent HASH heaped on thin toast, and it can go into individual greased casseroles to be baked in a 375° oven, with an egg carefully broken on top. It takes about 15 minutes, or until the egg is set, for this. Try STUFFED WHOLE GREEN PEPPERS—first hollowed and parboiled—filled with this mixture. Stand them upright in a deep, greased baking dish, pour canned or fresh stewed tomatoes almost to the top of the peppers, gently stir in a cup or two of cooked rice, bake ½ hour at 375°, and you have an easily prepared, toothsome, one-dish meal that can be contrived from leftovers.

VEAL À LA MAMA, whose origin I describe on page 162, feeds six when made with 1 pound of veal cutlet and 6 slices of peeled eggplant. Pound the cutlet with a potato masher for a few minutes, cut it and the eggplant into finger-length strips, dip them in a beaten egg, then bread crumbs, and quickly fry brown in cooking oil or lard. Sauté 1 cup of sliced onions in 2 tablespoons of butter until soft and put them into the bottom of a greased casserole. Place the cutlet and eggplant in layers on top. Stew 3 cups of canned or fresh tomatoes 15 minutes, add salt and pepper, a pinch of basil if you wish, thicken with 2 tablespoons of flour mixed with a little cold water, and pour gently over the contents of the casserole. Cover and bake in the oven at 375° for 45 minutes, or longer, with big scrubbed greased potatoes surrounding the casserole. Fifteen minutes before removing the casserole, add to it 1 cup of cooked string beans, peas, or asparagus tips, cover again, and finish in the oven.

BAKED HAM SLICE calls for a 1½ pound slice of smoked ham. Remove the rind and slash the edges of the fat. Cut 2 medium sweet potatoes into quarters lengthwise and parboil 5 minutes, in boiling salted water. Drain and brush with melted butter or cooking oil. Core 2 tart apples and cut into inch slices. Place the ham in a shallow greased baking dish, surround it with alternate slices of sweet potato and apple, and dust with ½ cup of brown sugar. Pour over ½ cup of water and bake in a 350° oven for 30 minutes. This serves six if your guests are not too hungry.

LAMB STEW for six. A steaming dish for a cold night. Cut up 3 pounds of shoulder or breast of lamb into 2-inch pieces. Brown in 3 tablespoons of fat; then cover with cold water and simmer for ½ hour. Add 8 small scraped carrots and 8 peeled onions, ½ cup of tomato juice, 1 teaspoon Worcestershire sauce, salt, pepper, and 1 tablespoon of chopped parsley. Cook 1 hour longer until the meat and vegetables are tender. Thicken the gravy a little with flour mixed with cold water. Have ready 1 cup of cooked peas. Serve the stew from a deep dish with the peas on top and pass with it buttered new potatoes boiled in their skins.

BRAISED STUFFED FLANK STEAK is so delicious that no one will guess or care about its low cost. A 1½ or 2 pound piece will feed four or six. Pound the meat for a few minutes with a wooden potato masher or meat mallet, and then pound ½ cup of flour, 1 teaspoon of salt, and a little pepper into each side. Crush 1 small clove of garlic, spear it with a toothpick, and let it remain in the pan while you melt ¼ cup of butter. Remove the garlic and add the butter to 2 cups of coarse bread crumbs with ¼ cup of finely chopped onion, 1 tablespoon of chopped parsley, and a pinch of thyme. Spread this stuffing on the steak and roll the meat loosely. Wrap 3 pieces of bacon around the roll and tie them with string so that the same fastening holds the meat together. You can use toothpicks but string stays put better. Brown the meat thoroughly in a very lightly greased skillet, and add 1 chopped carrot, a few celery leaves, ½ cup of tomato juice, ½ cup of water, and ½ cup of red wine. Cover the meat closely and simmer or bake in a slow oven until tender. Remove the meat to a hot platter and, if the gravy seems too greasy, skim off the fat before thickening it with 1 cup of sour cream and pouring over the meat.

Now, in honor of our British cousins, let's have BEEF AND KIDNEY PIE. Cut 1 pound of top of the round into inch cubes. Cover 2 beef kidneys with cold water and let soak for 1 hour. Cut them into inch cubes, discarding the core, and cover them with water and simmer 30 minutes. Drain and run cold water over them. Add to the cut-up beef, and dust with 4 tablespoons of flour. Melt 4 tablespoons of fat in a skillet, add the meat and 1 cup of chopped onions, and cook for 10 minutes, stirring frequently. Add 4 cups of canned consommé and water, half-and-half, salt, pepper, a pinch of thyme, 1 teaspoon of kitchen bouquet, and 1 teaspoon of Worcestershire sauce. Simmer 30 minutes. Line a deep baking dish with piecrust (page 117) and brush with the white of an egg. Pour in the meat and gravy. Wet the edges of the crust with water and cover with a top crust, pressing the edges well together. Cut two crossed slashes in the center. Bake in a 400° oven for 15 minutes, then reduce the heat to 350° and bake 30 minutes longer. It will stand baking 15 minutes more if you like. Serve to six or eight guests while still hot and bubbling.

VEAL AND HAM PIE takes a lot of doing but is the answer to that something different for a hot night. This recipe came from the chef of a small English liner, now sunk like so many of her gallant sisters. Cover a knuckle of veal with cold water, add 1 peeled onion, 1 clove, 1 teaspoon of parsley, and a scraped carrot. Bring slowly to a simmer and skim. Simmer for at least 2 hours; to get the meat really tender may take 3. Add 1 teaspoon of salt after 1 hour's cooking. Strain, and chop the meat coarsely, discarding all bits of gristle. Boil the broth down to 1 quart, taste for seasoning, cool, and skim off the fat. Chop coarsely 1 pound of lean, cooked, smoked ham. Slice 3 hard-boiled eggs. Beat 1 raw egg with 1 tablespoon of water, ½ teaspoon of salt, a shake of pepper, and a pinch each of savory and thyme. Add 1 cup of bread crumbs and form into balls the size of small marbles. Line a deep baking dish with piecrust and brush with the white of an egg. Then in an unhurried fashion—aren't the English leisurely?—loosely arrange the bits of veal, ham and hard-boiled egg in the dish, tucking the little bread-crumb dumplings into odd corners. Cover with a top crust as in the preceding recipe, but cut a small round hole in the center. Dissolve 1 teaspoon of granulated gelatine in the heated broth, place a small funnel in the hole in the crust, and carefully pour in just enough broth to cover the meat. Bake for 15 minutes in a 400° oven, then reduce the heat to 350° for another 30 minutes. Remove from the oven and, before cooling, funnel in enough of the still-warm broth to come up to the top of the crust. Chill for at least 8 hours, and your most Anglophobe guest will carol "There'll Always Be An England" with the first bite.

"You Don't Eat That?"

My family led a conventional existence; but while Father's bringing up had been that of a strict orthodox Friend, it was probably the age she lived in that restrained Mother's Irish blood from showing, except in a love of music, bright blue eyes, and an infectious always-ready laugh. Father declared that her attitude towards her constant bank overdrafts also displayed blarneying ancestry, and the only time I ever remember him speechless was when she guilelessly stated that of course any sensible trust company would allow its depositors occasional human errors on the wrong side of their balance sheets. Father heaved a weary sigh and gave up trying to teach Mother the principles of finance; thenceforward when the usual end-of-the-month phone call came to his office from her bank, his resigned "How much is it this time?" could be heard almost before "Dependable Trust speaking" ceased.

Otherwise my home followed the accepted Edwardian pattern of solid "handsome" furniture and lavish heavy meals. Father took charge of the carving and the wine cellar, while Mother ran the house and managed the three children, as well as the servants who each night willingly climbed four steep flights to an unheated, unplumbed attic which both she and they considered almost too luxurious.

From the start our married life dismayed my hitherto approving parents. Not only did we buy shabby antique furniture and allow our one hardworking servant unheard-of privileges, but my husband and I took our vacations in a twenty-foot sailboat which had no space for what Mother modestly referred to as a "bathroom." Worse was to come. Our second child and second wedding anniversary were almost simultaneous, and for some months before, I shame-facedly avoided Mother's shocked murmurs of "there must be peasant blood in your father's family," as she eyed my casually accepted and rapidly increasing girth. Instead, I frequently pushed the heavy gocart, on which our very young son sat enthroned on the day's marketing, into the small nearby Italian grocery and there took comfort from its ancient proprietress who regarded my suppos-edly disgraceful condition not only as natural but proper for a young married woman.

As the tinkle of the rusty shop bell died, the signora's beady eyes and toothless grin would appear from the littered backroom where she dwelt, surrounded by bottles of red wine, jars of homemade tomato paste, and a numerous family. "'Ello," she'd say. "Buy nice spaghetti today? You make a new bambino soon, yes? Fine!"

Once, after my purchases had been tied in the usual knobby newspaper bundle, she darted into her kitchen and reappeared with a piece of warm, brownish red pastry on a bright plate. "Eata," she beamed, "Good for you and dat new bambino." The first mouthful left dull, run-of-the-mill food without appeal forever, and I learned then never to scorn an odd-appearing dish: What I had been tempted with was ITALIAN TOMATO PIE, or PIZZA, and when I acquired the recipe we ate it frequently to increasing parental disapproval. As can be imagined, the original directions were garbled, but here is a clear set and its ingredients can be bought at any good American food store. Start by thickly greasing two 10 by 14 inch tin cooky sheets with olive oil in which a crushed clove of garlic has been sautéed and then removed. Next prepare the foundation of the pizzas and while an equal amount of bread dough can be used for this, the recipe below has the authentic olive oil flavor, doesn't call for very much of that hard-to-get and expensive shortening, and takes very little time to make. Put 1 cupful of lukewarm water into a bowl and add to it 1 tablespoon of olive oil, 1 tablespoon of sugar, 1 teaspoon of salt, and 1 crumbled yeast cake. Wait a minute for the yeast to soften, then beat in 3 or 4 cups of sifted flour to make a soft dough. Turn it out on a board or cloth, knead it for 5 or 6 minutes, using as little extra flour as possible, then put it back into its cleaned bowl, greasing it with 1 tablespoon of the oil. Cover and let rise in a warm place until doubled in bulk. This will only take about an hour, and like other doughs it can be punched down after rising and kept covered in the icebox until wanted. Cut the dough in half and roll each piece until it fits a cooky sheet. This is the only difficult part of the proceeding, as it takes patience and some practice to get the dough to the desired thinness, but persevere in pulling and rolling, making a ½-inch high dam of dough around the edge of each tin. Cover the dough with thin slices of Provalona cheese, first removing the rind—about ½ pound or a little more, depending upon the thinness of the slices. Thin 4 cans of Italian tomato paste with 2 tablespoons of olive oil and 2 cups of canned consommé or chicken broth, and spread this over the cheese. Drain 2 cans of flat anchovy fillets and lay them on the tomato paste in hollow squares or any other design your fancy dictates. A half-pound of salted Italian anchovies can be substituted here, but while their flavor may be better they must first be soaked for 5 minutes before being drained and boned. Let the pies rest and rise in a warm place for 1 hour; then into a 375° oven for 20 minutes until the edges are crisp and brown and the filling a mass of savory-smelling bubbling richness. Each pizza should feed four or six and they are easiest served right from the hot tin with the old family pie knife; any leftover will disappear from the refrigerator with surprising speed. Slices of ripe olives and bits of peeled mushrooms can be added to the sauce and a little sweet basil for a really authentic flavor. Extra garlic and onion, too, if you wish, and if the directions seem vague remember that this is a dish as happy-go-lucky as its originators in their pre-Mussolini days. Hot or cold, with a green salad and a flask of not-too-sour Chianti, it has it all over Omar's bottle and meager loaf, even in solitude needing no book of verses to make it good eating. When during the war our son discovered that his ship's Italian cook had worked in a pizzeria, the pleas that crossed the Pacific for the canned salt fish must have caused censors to feel that Operation Anchovy was only second in importance to the atomic bomb.

A two-generation devotion to that youthful classic gave the name of "Swiss Family Potter Picnics" to our numerous outings with the children, and every clear Sunday for years "Mother" filled her "wonderful bag" with otherwise forgotten articles, our son, alias "Ernst," stowed food in the car, aided by a very feminine "Jack," while "Father," true to form, stood leisurely by directing all the labor. A trip which had as its objective a rocky ledge some miles from our summer cottage remains in memory because on that particular morning Father and Mother, unlike their less convivial Swiss prototypes, were suffering the effects of a late and much-too-gay clambake the night before. None the less a promise was a promise, so grill, beefsteak, potatoes, milk, cake and fruit were packed in the old Ford and off we went. Arrived at our destination, Father built a big driftwood fire, set up the grill, and with the *sotto voce* remark that sleep was much more necessary to his continued existence than food, stretched out in the warm sun. Meanwhile the children clambered happily around the rocky pools below, returning at all-too-frequent intervals to show their apathetic parents some fresh treasure in the way of a dead crab or an equally odoriferous shell. Suddenly, after a welcome silence there came loud shouts of "Mother! Come quick," and I bumped in panic down the rocks to the water's edge, certain that my darlings were being attacked by a herd of hungry octopi, at least.

But Ernst and Jack had read the book to more purpose than their elders, and the bed of mussels they had discovered at high-tide mark made the day memorable for a second time. We pulled big fistfuls, trimmed their beards with Ernst's grimy pocketknife, and washed the shells well with cool seawater. Then, as we were wondering what to cook them on, came the discovery of a piece of rusty corrugated roofing resting on a nearby rock. With renewed belief in fictional Swiss findings, the iron was set over the grill, the mussels arranged on top, and by the time the heat had opened them up we had butter melted to go with each morsel, supping them from their shells with delighted *whooshes*, and shortly a much revived Father and Mother were able—just as in the book—to bore Ernst and Jack by pointing out the proverbial advantages of always keeping their eyes open.

Mussels, almost unknown on this side of the Atlantic except as bait, can be purchased in many seafood markets and are well worth a trial by any family, Swiss or American. Good just as we prepared them on the beach, they are at their best and most famous as MOULES MARINIÈRE. For four or six, wash 2 quarts of mussels in several waters and trim their fringy edges with sharp kitchen shears. Have ready a saucepan of sufficient size and put in it ½ cup of dry white wine, 1 or 2 chopped cloves of garlic, ½ cup of chopped parsley, an optional bit of chopped celery, and ¼ cup of butter. As with oysters, no salt should be needed, but a few twirls of the pepper grinder won't be amiss. Put in the mussels, cover the saucepan closely, and set it over a hot fire for 5 minutes, after which remove the lid and see whether the mussels have opened. If not, continue steaming until they do open. Serve them hot in big soup plates or deep bowls, with their redolent juice. Fingers—and finger bowls—are the only utensils devotees demand for the enjoyment of this insufficiently known delight, with perhaps a thick slice of warm French bread for postoperative dunking. Silence those finicky souls who call for spoons by superiorly scooping up the few last precious drops of your own luscious sauce in one of the empty shells.

Sometimes out-of-town friends have deemed us inhospitable when their unexpected phone calls haven't always been followed by our usually enthusiastic invitation to dinner, but bitter experience has taught us the uninterested answer that comes back at the mention of calf's brains as the planned meal, although amusingly the same people have been known to display foreign menus with pride while discoursing on the epicurean delights of *cervelle au beurre noir*. So if you too, feel hesitant at the first thought, pretend to be in some famous French restaurant where an obsequious garçon is offering this delicate *plat* for certain approval.

CALF'S BRAINS WITH BLACK BUTTER. Allow 1 set of brains—or more, for true addicts—for each serving. Soak the brains in cold water for 1 hour or so and drain. Add 1 sliced onion, a bit of chopped parsley and celery, 1 tablespoon of salt, and ½ cup of vinegar to enough boiling water to cover the brains, and simmer them gently for ½ hour. Drain and when cool tenderly remove the skin and any bits of bone the butcher may have left clinging to their surface. For each 2 sets of brains melt ½ cup of butter (or as much more as can be spared) in a shallow pan and allow it to brown slightly. Add the brains and cook over a medium high heat for 20 minutes, or until each side is covered with a light brown crust. Remove to a hot serving dish. Increase the heat if the butter hasn't already reached a beautiful dark brown, and add 1 tablespoon of sharp vinegar and an optional tablespoon of capers. Pour this over the brains with a little chopped parsley and serve. This is a dish that calls for real butter, so if there is a shortage of the dairy product, prepare the brains for cooking as directed, brown them in the smallest amount of butter possible, and pour over them the white wine gravy on page 96. CERVELLE AU VIN BLANC is what you'll be enjoying.

A usually unheeded sense of thrift was the cause of my learning to prepare a calf's head. The marketing pocketbook was woefully thin and company was on its way, but at a very low cost four delighted guests sat down to a main dish of MOCK TERRAPIN. Appeal to the butcher to split a calf's head and remove the brains. (You already know what to do with them.) Soak the head in cold water for 1 hour, then drain and cover with fresh water. Add 2 teaspoons of salt, a sprig of parsley, and 1 sliced onion. A stalk of celery and a few peppercorns too, if you have them. Simmer gently until the meat is tender—about 2 hours—then drain and cool. Reserve the tongue for a dish that comes later, for you are working on a truly economical section of the animal. Cut the head meat into 1 inch pieces. Hard boil, shell and slice 3 eggs. Melt 1 tablespoon of butter in the top of a double boiler. Blend in 1 tablespoon of flour and slowly add 3 cups of thin cream or top milk, 1 teaspoon of salt, ½ teaspoon of dry mustard, and a dash of cayenne. When it thickens slightly add the meat and sliced eggs and let everything become piping hot. Meantime, beat the yolks of 2 eggs with 2 tablespoons each of dry sherry and cream. Stir this into the hot meat and its sauce, bring back to the original temperature, and serve immediately. Spoons as well as forks should accompany this, and big baked potatoes.

CALF'S HEAD CHEESE, a grand hot-weather snack, has the meat cooked until very tender, then coarsely chopped, mixed with a tiny scrape of onion, 1 teaspoon of salt, the same amount of poultry seasoning and chopped parsley, and an optional shake of cayenne. While still warm, press it into a greased mould, right up to the top, cover it tightly, and chill overnight before unmoulding it on a bed of watercress garnished with crimson sliced tomatoes.

STEWED CALF'S HEAD I found interleaved into a very old cookbook. On the back of the yellowed paper is written in a copperplate hand, "June, 1837. Give this to Helen." These are the original instructions with modern parentheses. Boil your (?) head till the bones can be removed, then take out the bones and lay it on a dish to drain. Put your butter, a piece as big as an egg (2 tablespoons), onto the fire, and when hot lay your head in and let it brown a little, first having seasoned it with salt (1 teaspoon), pepper (¼ teaspoon), and a little allspice and cloves (a pinch each). Take it out and lay it on your dish. Take a lump of butter the size of a walnut

(2 teaspoons), dust some flour (1½ tablespoons) over it, and let it brown. Put in a little (½ cup) water (or diluted consommé) and add to your gravy ½ dozen cloves, as many whole allspice, and a tumblerful (1 cup) of wine (sherry). Let them all simmer together (until thickened), then strain and pour over the meat. Chop 2 hard-boiled eggs, strew over the dish, and garnish with lemon.

The CALF'S TONGUE unfortunately won't serve more than two or three at most but it is so delicious—and cheap—that an extra tongue or two is worth the purchase. Cook them as directed above (Mock Terrapin), let cool, skin, and remove any bone. Cover them with red wine gravy (page 96) made with the water in which they were boiled. Add 2 peeled carrots and a few tiny peeled onions for each serving and place in a tightly covered casserole in a 375° oven for 1½ hours. BRAISED TONGUE is the result and very good it is.

The title should be sufficient directions, but for TONGUE AND MUSHROOMS cut the prepared cooked tongue into thin slices, allow ½ cup of sliced mushrooms for each tongue, and sauté both in 2 tablespoons of butter for 5 minutes. Blend in 2 tablespoons of flour and let it brown a little. Slowly stir in 2 cups of the water in which the tongue or head was boiled. Simmer, stirring, until creamy and then add 1 tablespoon of dry sherry and 1 teaspoon of Worcestershire sauce, a shake of cayenne, and extra salt if necessary. A TONGUE HASH made as on page 54, is by no means to be scorned either, you'll find.

The water in which the calf's head is boiled makes an easily jellied but rather tasteless soup. Either use it with the addition of ½ pound of chopped raw beef as in the base for vegetable soup (page 39), or flavor it with beef extract, bouillon cubes, or canned consommé, before serving it clear, hot or cold.

Altogether, a calf's head is well worth experimenting with and not only for economy. Imagination is the only limit to the ways of serving it, and once started you'll not wonder at my reaction when, during meat rationing, I saw a Helen Hokinson type ordering the last one in the store for "cat food," and had to be forcibly restrained from murder.

EELS we learned perforce to eat during a fishing trip to out-of-the-way Chincoteague Island. Early spring had brought the famous ponies out in appealing groups, comfortable rooms we had, even indoor plumbing, although "the bathtub had been lent to the minister," for what purpose we never discovered; but the sport we had come for was woefully lacking. Morning after morning we hopefully put off-shore in our small boat, to return in the late afternoon with heavy coats of sunburn and empty baskets. We dined at the town's only eatery and in a week its menu of panned, fried, roast or stewed oysters began to pall on even such addicts of the bivalve as we. Meat was scarce, the proprietor apologized, but he would be only too glad to cook and serve any of our catch. Laughing hollowly in every meaning of the word, we were forced to admit that our only catch so far had been eels, not to be eaten, of course, but unhooked with loathing and thrown back in the water. When he insisted that "eels was de bes' eatin' on de Sho'" we brought him some of the unattractive things and bade him do his best or eat his words and the horrible creatures as well. We were the ones who did both. The eels arrived at our table crisp and brown and were devoured in a silence almost devout. FRIED EELS. First, unless of a really hardy nature, have the eels skinned and beheaded well out of sight. Then remove the backbone and cut into convenient lengths. Four inches is a nice size. Beat 1 whole egg with 2 tablespoons of water or white wine. Put 1 cup of bread crumbs on a plate and mix with it 1 teaspoon of salt and the same of black pepper. Dip the sections of eel in the egg and then roll in the crumbs. Have ready a skillet in which a half-inch of bacon fat is smoking. Fry until each side is a delicate tan; 10 minutes should do it. Drain carefully and serve on a hot plate with slices of lemon or lemon butter (page 97).

SAUTÉED EELS are the fillets cooked in a very little butter to which 1 crushed clove of garlic has been added. Remove the garlic and add a teaspoon of white wine and a little chopped parsley for each serving.

"BOILT AALS" came from a very ancient English cookbook. King Alfred undoubtedly enjoyed them when he wasn't busy burning cakes and ruining dinner. Sauté 1 tablespoon of chopped onion—or 2 of chopped chives—in 2 tablespoons of butter until the onion starts to color. Add 1 tablespoon of chopped parsley, 2 cups of red wine, 2 teaspoons of vinegar, 1 teaspoon of salt, a shake of pepper, and another of cayenne. The original calls for a pinch of nutmeg, too, but that's optional. When the wine simmers, gently slide in 3 pounds of filleted eel. Cover and continue simmering for ½ hour, then remove the eel to a warm plate and let the sauce boil for 2 or 3 minutes longer. Blend 2 teaspoons of butter with 2 teaspoons of flour, thin this with a little of the hot wine, and slowly stir it into the rest. Simmer and stir for 10 minutes, then pour it over the eels. "Serve with sippets of toste." The red wine seems contrary to all the principles of fish cookery but the result here is a hearty succulent dish, and after all, *are* eels fish?

Against tripe I fought a long but losing battle, and like many another of the defeated, now bless the victor. In the city I was accustomed and always indifferent to my husband's weekly remark, "Tripe for lunch today," swearing that nothing would ever get me to taste, much less cook, the horrid-looking stuff. But when we moved to the country, miles from the nearest restaurant, his hints anent his favorite dish grew so insistent that it became a question of tripe or divorce, and for a short time it was a difficult decision. The "winnah" was tripe creole, much better than a trip to Reno.

In all of the following recipes, except where noted, prepare the tripe as follows: Allow 1 pound per person, as it shrinks unbelievably in cooking. The honeycomb variety is supposed to be best but English and French cookbooks—and they should know—say that the "double fold" has the finer flavor. Either, or a mixture of both, is good. Soak the tripe in cold water for 1 hour, then cover it with fresh water and rub it between your hands just as though scrubbing the bath towel it so much resembles. This is more fun than it sounds. Now cover the tripe with water once again, add 1 sliced onion, a few peppercorns, a sprig of parsley, and bring to a boil. Cover and let simmer until very tender. To my surprise most cookbooks allow only one hour for this, but I find it always takes at least 3 hours for the tripe to reach the stage we consider perfection. Tell when it's done by lifting a piece from the kettle with a fork, and when a sharp knife cuts through it easily, call it a day. Drain and cool. This will keep, well covered, for at least 2 or 3 days, so is one more of those handy things that can be prepared well ahead.

TRIPE CREOLE. Cut the tripe into pieces about the width and half the length of a lead pencil and let it get very hot in the creole sauce (page 95). Serve it with lots of boiled rice.

FRIED TRIPE. Beat 1 egg with 2 teaspoons of water or white wine. Season 1 cup of bread crumbs with 1 teaspoon of salt and the same of pepper. Dip the tripe, cut into squares or strips, first in the egg and then in the crumbs, and fry until brown in hot fat or cooking oil, turning each side if necessary. Drain on brown paper and serve plain or with white wine gravy (page 96), or tomato sauce (page 181).

Broiled tripe we ate first at a little Canadian hotel, entirely surrounded by retired "Colonel Blimps" and their lorgnette-carrying wives. Even the cotton-stockinged waitresses had that distantly high-nosed air generally associated with royalty, and when I humbly asked if I could have another serving of the meat, to be answered with a sniffy "Yes, modom, you may," I felt put in my place by an expert. But the typically British food was much better than usual and the BROILED TRIPE superb. Dip palm-sized slices of cooked tripe in cooking oil or melted butter. Let drain a little and brown quickly under a hot broiler. This was served with plain boiled potatoes— Oh, those English!—and creamed onions, and it is such a fine combination that I am willing at any moment to join in "The Maple Leaf Forever."

TRIPE À LA MODE DE CAEN us the final chord in this symphony. For six, wash, but do not cook, 6 pounds of tripe and cut it into comfortable-sized pieces. Butter a deep casserole, a big one with an inset tight-fitting lid. Put 2 slices of chopped bacon and 1 calf or pig foot (have the butcher crack it) in the bottom. Add the tripe and scatter around it 1 cup each of sliced carrot and onion, 2 chopped garlic cloves, 1 chopped celery stalk, a sprig of parsley, half a bay leaf, a pinch of thyme, and a whole clove. Add ½ cup of skinned and chopped tomatoes, or the same amount of canned, and pour in 1 cup of dry white wine and 1 cup of good brandy. This last adds to the expense but the tripe is correspondingly cheap. Add enough canned consommé or chicken broth to cover the meat, taste for salt, add a grind of pepper, and put on the lid. Now go back to childhood, mix almost 1 cup of thick flour-and-water paste, and seal the casserole with this. Bake it in a 275°–300° oven for 6 to 8 hours according to your convenience, and serve hot and bubbling from the dish it was cooked in. Some cooks say to open the casserole and remove the few bones before serving, but this loses the glorious fine flourish with which the host or hostess should cut the hard paste seal, and also deprives the anxiously awaiting guests of their rightful first whiff of the deservedly classic repast. Serve with buttered boiled potatoes and a green salad. With iced white wine also on the table, could there be a more perfect meal?

The law courts were closed on Election Day and early that clear November morning my attorney-husband and I cast our canceling votes for opposing "right parties" and started off for a whole day's exploring of the Pennsylvania Dutch countryside. Witch signs were our passion of the moment. Finally, we arrived at Intercourse—yes, there is just such a town, find it on the map—whence we gleefully mailed unsigned but postmarked cards saying, of course, "Wish you were here," to various friends none of whom knew we were in that part of the state. Ah, Youth! Then, exhausted by this attempt at humor and blackmail, we looked for a place to eat. The first two we tried were firmly closed; they take their politics and religions seriously in those regions. The third would serve us if we would eat the family dinner. Would we! The traditional sweets and sours were already on the table and we dove right into—hold your breath, now—pickled beets, pickled cucumbers, mustard and green tomato pickle, catsup, spiced and pickled peaches, old-fashioned cole slaw, apple butter, strawberry jam, quince honey, and, as the country auction sheets say, "other articles too numerous to mention," coming up for air just as the waiter bore in a big steaming tureen of lusciously sauced meat and staggered in a minute later under an equally large plate of country fried potatoes. Words were inadequate, but when our Ganymede appeared with deep-dish apple pie and about a pound of bitey cheese we had recovered sufficiently to ask the name of the stew. A gargled "Rwpt" was the reply and it wasn't until halfway home that I gave a tardy scream of comprehension.

Our colored cook heard the story and offered to provide a recipe for equally good FRICASSEED RABBIT. If possible, have the butcher split the rabbit down the back and disjoint it, although it is really just as easy to do at home as to divide a chicken. Do not wash it unless necessary. Dust the pieces with seasoned flour—1 teaspoon of salt, 1 teaspoon of pepper to each cup. Remove the rind of ¼ pound of fat salt pork and cut into small dice. Place it in a skillet over medium heat and when the meat yellows add the cut-up rabbit. Increase the heat slightly and cook, turning each piece until well browned and crusty. Stir in 2 tablespoons of the seasoned flour and let it brown a little, too. Slowly add 3 cups of water and let simmer until it starts to thicken. In another smaller pan melt 2 tablespoons of butter and brown the liver and ½ cup of chopped onion in this, mashing the liver as finely as possible. Add this to the rabbit, cover closely, and simmer until the rabbit is tender, about 1½ or 2 hours. Plain baked sweet potatoes are good with this.

Rabbit can also be cooked as in Beef à la Mode Sentimentale (page 48) for a very superior HASSENPFEFFER. Boiled noodles and beer are the side dishes here, and a rigid sense of poetic justice demands peas as well as lettuce, Peter and his family being such ruthless despoilers of both greens.

My "French" artist-uncle raved about COCKSCOMBS WITH WINE, but it took wartime rationing and an adjacent chicken farm before I attempted them. By that time the word had gone out via the country grapevine that I

was writing a book and my mad request was just an anticlimax. The combs were saved each week when dressing the fowls for market, frozen in the refrigerator, and when there was a drawerful we invited appreciative gourmets to share them. Two cups will feed four people. Rinse the combs in water, drain, cover with fresh water—about 2 more cups—add 1 teaspoon of salt and a twist of the pepper grinder, and simmer 5 minutes or so, until tender. Drain and reduce the broth to 1 cup. Melt 2 tablespoons of butter in a skillet, add 1 teaspoon of finely minced celery and the same amount of minced parsley and scraped onion. Green onion tops or chives are better if you have them, for this is a delicate dish. Let them cook over a moderate heat for 5 minutes, then add 2 tablespoons of flour. When this bubbles, add the broth and 1½ cups of dry sauterne or light claret. Not the heavier Burgundy, for it kills the flavor. Simmer and stir until creamy, add the cockscombs, allow them to get thoroughly hot, and serve surrounded with toast points. We eat boiled rice and the usual green salad with this, although there may be more traditional accompaniments. But Uncle Charlie is now painting his pictures for an undoubtedly appreciative heavenly host, and lacking his encouragement here on earth, my French has descended to that of the scole of Stratford-atte-Bowe.

Convinced by now, I hope, that strange foods are not only edible, but delicious and often economical, continue your culinary explorations by searching out of the way delicatessens and hole-in-the-wall groceries for more of that something different. Put unsuccessful buys down to experience but there will be many more on the credit than the debit side. Italian stores sell herbs, sausages and cheeses that are well worth a try, as are kosher breads, pickled meats and fish, while coarse kosher salt is far more flavorful than any always-pouring iodized brand. French and Swedish groceries need no recommendation, and oh, if the German nation would concentrate only on such activities as putting more caraway seed in their pumperknickel! Even a crossroads general emporium may prove a gold mine. One tiny seashore grocery carries our favorite canned baked lima beans that superior city merchants refuse to stock, and its fisherman proprietor salts or smokes part of his catch for our year-round breakfasts. A small store in a little New York town supplies us with delicious hams.

Explore strange as well as familiar neighborhoods for eating places, too. The cop on his beat or the gas station attendant can often give better advice than roadside signs of Tea Shoppes or a book on Good Eating. We go miles out of our way to dine in a grimy coal town whose spotless restaurant was first recommended by a Polish policeman and where childish wails of "Don't go down the mine, Daddy!" must be unknown, for the workers descend to their labors fortified by the most tremendous orders of heavenly boiled beef and featherlight dumplings.

The best Italian spaghetti I ever tasted was eaten, surprisingly, in a screened white tent strategically situated between the bingo game and the kitchen-gadget demonstration at an upstate Ohio country fair. We faithfully returned each day of the fair for all three attractions. Language difficulties made attempts to learn the spaghetti recipe unsuccessful but we were finally beckoned into the tiny cubbyhole where the Patronna cooked tomato sauce over a minute oil-burning stove, and after unintelligible compliments both sides drank toasts to international cooking and unity, in homemade red wine.

Many references to difficult-to-get herbs and other seasonings have been purposely left out of this book, for while they may add interest to a new recipe they more often interfere with its attempting. As to the depressing and too frequently recurring call for "shallots" in many cookbooks, take cheer. Again, from experience, I know that few can tell the difference between shallots and a small scrape of mild onion—and the screams of epicures, including those of my French hairdresser, fall on deaf ears as I write. Tantalized for years by this impossible-to-buy ingredient, I finally commanded sets of the bulbs at a high price from a swank New York seedsman, not a whit dismayed when the order was followed by a request for the name of our "Estate Manager." On our Maryland farm they flourished like the wild onions they so much resemble, and each spring the fall's forgotten bulblets produced a lush new crop. Now they are used only to impress visiting gourmets, most of whom have to be told whence comes the familiar flavor.

So go your culinary ways with confidence and without apology. Use only one standard in trying out strange foods or seasonings: that you like the result. Follow a new recipe exactly, the first time it is tried, but after that add individual touches unafraid, lightheartedly paying little attention to my or anyone else's instructions except as they appeal to your particular taste.

Hard-Shelled Ancestors
and Their Finny Friends

We had spent a happy weekend motoring through Maryland's lovely Eastern Shore, crossing into Virginia and braving miles of dirt road to see the spot where one of my forebears is buried under an imposing block of sculptured stone. Ancestor or not, a horrid man he was, for even though Mrs. Custis may have been a poor cook, no wife, whatever her faults, could merit his revengeful epitaph:

> BENEATH THIS MARBLE TOMB LIES YE BODY
> OF THE HONORABLE JOHN CUSTIS, ESQ.,
> OF THE CITY OF WILLIAMSBURG
> AND THE PARISH OF BRUTON.
> AGE 71 YEARS AND YET LIVED BUT SEVEN YEARS
> WHICH WAS THE SPACE OF TIME
> HE KEPT A BACHELOR'S HOME AT ARLINGTON.

After days of dull food at roadside stands we turned north, first stopping at an ancient wharf and coming gleefully away with a burlap bag containing a half-bushel of big salt oysters and some three dozen equally large clams. Then off again, our mouths watering at the thought of the visit ahead to our friend Kitty Higgins, who is not only a marvelous cook but shares with our own daughter-in-law the distinction of being one of the most skillful female oyster openers in the Chesapeake Bay country. A talent it is, and almost as rare in the sex as the ability to handle a hammer.

The first night's meal included "Roasts" as well as "Raws" and the flavor of ROAST OYSTERS is so subtle that I wonder more people don't use the backyard grills that are springing up all over the country, for their simple preparation. Outdoors or in, the directions are the same. We did ours in the living room where a glowing fire kept off the autumn chill, but a housewife less interested in the delicious result might object to the accompanying mess. But if you don't mind the mess, let the fire burn down to a mass of red coals, put the well-scrubbed oysters, deep shell down, on a grill over the fire, and when the shells open, off the oysters must come. Look out, they're hot! Cold beer or ale is the drink with them, and the true Eastern Shore roast-oyster addict doesn't want his attention distracted from the business in hand by any foolish side dishes of vegetables or salad. Once he has on the heavy gloves that help him get the hot beauties off the grill, he simply goes to work with a fork and a saucer of melted butter.

The next night our hostess produced SCALLOPED OYSTERS and the delights of the earlier meal were almost forgotten. Her recipe is an old one, accounting for its lavish use of butter—worthwhile here you'll admit—and was for forty, yes, you heard me correctly, forty people. There was certainly real hospitality, as well as lots of butter, long ago. The recipe ends with the admonition to bake only enough at one time for a single serving all around, so if you're going to feed more than the four people which the modernized version calls for, make at least two dishes. Even with the smaller number it is not a bad idea to cook the oysters in shifts, for they must be very hot and fresh from the oven to be at their best. Have 1 quart of large freshly opened oysters, not, if you can help it, the little tasteless "stewers" that are ladled up loose from a messy bowl or can. That's what caterers use, along with a doughy sauce, and it accounts, I'm sure, for the bad name this originally succulent dish has acquired. Drain off their juice and pick the oysters over carefully to remove every bit of shell. Put a thick coating of butter on a casserole that will hold 3 or 4 layers of the bivalves and dust it well with coarse bread crumbs. Homemade crumbs are the best, but grocery-bought will do. Then a layer of oysters, a grind of the pepper mill, ¼ cup of butter cut into small pieces, and the least scraping, say ⅛ teaspoon, of onion. Then another thin layer of crumbs. Keep on with oysters, crumbs, onion and butter until the casserole is full. Make the last layer crumbs with an extra dose of butter. An old-fashioned recipe if ever there was one. Then into a 400° oven for 15 or 20 minutes until the top is just brown and the oysters have given their flavorsome juice to every bit of the dish. Don't worry about the lack of salt, really fresh oysters need very little of that seasoning. We had asparagus salad with vinaigrette dressing with this dish, and warm French bread, and for dessert a compote of fruit with homemade cake. We were a satisfied houseful.

Although I must give her the credit for showing me the simple way to open the shells, the DEVILED CLAMS we ate before we left are a combination of Kitty's and my recipes with the best points of each. Take 30 large clams and put them into a pot the bottom of which is barely covered with water. Clap on the lid and let them steam until they start to open. This takes a surprisingly short time, so keep your eye on the pot and get the clams off the heat when the edges of the shells show just the smallest crack. Run a thin-bladed sharp knife down between the opened shells and out comes the clam. Do this over a bowl to save every drop of the precious juice and put the water from the pot into the bowl, too. Pick over the clams just as you did the oysters, then run them through the food chopper, using the medium cutter. It is a messy job but the only way to get the tough parts fit to eat. (Two tablespoons of the chopped clams can go in with the strained juice and all reserved for clam bisque, page 42, if you like.) Put 6 slices of hard stale bread, 1 small peeled onion, and 2 stalks of parsley through the chopper after the clams, or use 1½ cups of bread crumbs. Mix everything together with a pinch or two of thyme, but not too much of the herb or you'll destroy that clam flavor. The mixture should be just thick enough to hold its shape and if it seems too solid add a little clam juice. Like those with flour, recipes with bread crumbs are hard to standardize. Take 12 of the largest and deepest clamshells, or shallow individual casseroles, or one big baking dish, grease them well, pile in the clam mixture and sprinkle the tops with more crumbs and a few bits of butter. Prop the shells up straight in a shallow pan and bake in a 375° oven until the crumbs are brown.

BOILED ROCK FISH is another famous Eastern Shore recipe and any firm-fleshed fish is good prepared the same way. Buy a 3-pound one—the little babies don't respond so well to the treatment—and have it cleaned but leave the head and tail on. Sew it up in cheesecloth or any clean cloth, even a piece of Daddy's discarded shirt will do. Wrap the fish loosely and sew the material together with coarse thread and big stitches. Put it on a rack in a fish boiler or any big pot that will let it stretch out full length. Cover with boiling water, add 1 sliced onion, salt and pepper, and let it simmer 30 minutes. At this point you will feel that you are working on an ex-member of the Ku Klux Klan and no one will blame you. Melt 2 tablespoons of butter over a medium heat, add 2 tablespoons of flour, blend, and stir in slowly 1 cup of water from the fish and 1 cup of thin cream or top milk. Cook slowly until thickened and add 2 tablespoons of capers, 1 tablespoon of the caper vinegar, and 1 tablespoon of white wine. Keep this CAPER SAUCE hot. Take out the fish carefully—a cake turner in each hand does this job if you can't find a willing assistant. Put it on a hot platter and with equal care unroll it from its wrapping. Be gay and put a ribbon of green pepper or pimento around its neck. Cover the fish with half the sauce and serve the rest from a gravy boat. This is that rare dish that is equally good for lunch, dinner, or a hearty breakfast.

SCALLOPS IN WHITE WINE are a welcome change from the eternal overfried nubbins that seem to be the beginning and end of this seafood to most people. For four people order 1 pound, or better yet 1½ pounds. Melt 4 tablespoons of butter in an iron skillet, add the scallops, and stir over a medium heat until they acquire a tempting golden hue, then remove them from the pan and keep them comfortable in a hot serving dish. Scrape every bit of essence up from the bottom of the pan and add 1 tablespoon of flour and that little scrape of onion that I keep harping on. Put it back on the fire and when the flour starts to bubble slowly stir in 1½ cups of dry white wine and salt and pepper to taste. Let it cook 10 minutes longer and pour over the scallops.

SCALLOPED FISH for four calls for 2 cups of boiled flaked fish, 3 sliced hard-boiled eggs, and 3 cups of white sauce (page 94). Arrange the fish—canned, freshly cooked, or leftover—with the eggs in a greased casserole, pour the white sauce over, dust the top with bread crumbs, dot it with butter, a little extra salt and pepper, and bake at 375° until brown. Cooked peas instead of the eggs makes this a FISH WIGGLE. What a name! Add 2 tablespoons of sherry to the sauce and call it POISSON AUX POIS.

SALMON PROVINCIAL is made with inch-thick unskinned steaks of the fish, dipped in oil and laid in a shallow buttered pan that has been well rubbed with a cut clove of garlic after greasing. Brown them quickly under a broiler, turn carefully, brown the other side. Place the fish on a hot platter. Heat 1 tablespoon of butter and 1 teaspoon of white wine for each slice, in the same pan. Add a little chopped parsley and pour over the fish before serving.

SALMON MOUSSE for four or six can be made with either freshly boiled or canned fish. Bone 1 pound of whichever kind you choose and put it through the fine cutter of the meat grinder. Add ½ cup of bread crumbs previously soaked in 1½ cups of thin cream. Season with salt and pepper, mix the mass well, and chill thoroughly, overnight if you wish. Add the stiffly beaten whites of 6 eggs and put it into a greased mould. Set it in a shallow pan of water and bake at 375° for 45 minutes. A fish-shaped mould is appropriate, but it tastes just as well cooked in an oblong bread pan. Turn it out and serve with 2 cups of hot white sauce (page 94) to which have been added ½ cup of crab meat or sautéed chopped mushrooms and 1 tablespoon of sherry.

My own CRAB IMPERIAL takes time but only one saucepan for its preparation. Cut 4 large green peppers in half lengthwise, remove the seeds and white ribs, and parboil them 5 minutes. Drain and set them in a greased baking dish. Pick over 1 pound of lump crab meat and mix it with 2 tablespoons of white wine and a squeeze of lemon juice. Melt 2 tablespoons of butter in the empty saucepan, blend in 1½ tablespoons of flour, and stir in slowly 1½ cups of thin cream or top milk. Add salt, pepper, 1 teaspoon each of chopped chives and parsley, 1 tablespoon of Worcestershire sauce, 1 teaspoon of dry mustard, a pinch of cayenne and a pinch of nutmeg. Mix in the crab meat and add 1 chopped hard-boiled egg. Pile into the peppers, sprinkle with bread crumbs, and bake for 10 or 15 minutes in a 400° oven.

BAKED SHAD HOLLANDAISE. Season the inside of a cleaned 3-pound shad with salt and pepper. Brush with melted butter or oil and bake in a 400° oven for 30 minutes. Remove it carefully to a hot platter, cover it with hollandaise sauce (page 97), and quickly run it close up under a very hot broiler until the sauce just begins to brown. Serve it immediately. Any large baked fish is good in this fashion but you'll find the shad something extra. Be sure not to use your best silver platter, or you're likely to end up with a blob of metal in the bottom of the oven and, worse than that, no dinner.

SHRIMPS FLORENTINE for four can also be made with cooked flaked fish or crab meat, and if cooked asparagus tips are the foundation you'll have to name the dish yourself. Chop finely 2 cups of cooked spinach, add salt and pepper, a scrape of onion, and a tiny pinch of nutmeg. Spread it in a buttered baking dish. Cook 1 pound of shrimps 20 minutes in boiling salted water. Drain and remove the heads, tails, shells and black back vein, and then arrange the shrimps on top of the spinach. Cover with 2 cups of well-seasoned white sauce (page 94) to which has been added 2 tablespoons of white wine. Dust with bread crumbs and 1 teaspoon of grated Parmesan cheese. Swiss cheese can also be used. Dot with butter, shake on a dash of paprika, and bake in a 400° oven for 15 minutes.

When next you see high-priced FILET OF SOLE MARGUERY on the menu of a swank restaurant, don't be depressed and count your pennies. Make it at home yourself, instead. For four people take 4 medium-sized filets of flounder, 2 or 2½ pounds altogether, and cut each piece in half. Put in a shallow saucepan, just cover with dry white wine, add 2 slices of onion, salt and a few peppercorns, and let them simmer gently 10 minutes. Drain the fish well, and put it on a hot platter in a cosy spot. Boil the wine until it measures ½ cup. Beat the yolks of 2 eggs until light, then gradually add the hot strained wine. Put the eggs and wine in the top of a small double boiler over very hot but not strenuously boiling water. Continue beating, and slowly add ½ cup of butter cut in pieces. When the sauce is just thick pour it over the fish and dust the top with 1 teaspoon of Parmesan cheese. Run it quickly under a very hot broiler to color, and serve it immediately.

Now we come to the famous Filet-of-Sole-Marguery Controversy, in the heat of which gourmets call each other names in cookbook French and the fur—or rather the fish—starts to fly. One school of chefs insists that the defenseless cooked fish be decorated with bits of boiled shrimp, mushrooms, clams, mussels, lobster, and truffles. The other, with just as many cordons bleus to back it up, stands for the fish as God made it, or rather, as it came from the oven with only the golden cheese-flavored sauce as a covering. Either way is delectable but old friends have been known to quarrel and part unreconciled on the subject. Perhaps it was just such an argument that sent John Custis, embittered, to his Virginia grave, and if his wife had only served him SOLE TURBANE in which each flounder filet is toothpicked around a cooked shelled shrimp, simmered in wine and finished with a plain sauce made just as in the preceding recipe, my hot-tempered ancestor might have enjoyed a peaceful dinner table, an almost identical dish, and a happy married life.

Greens from the Ground Up

F our years of country living have taught me many things, among them the certainty that the gold brick was sold by, and not to, the farmer. Our rustic landlady guilelessly accepted a high city rent for a rundown farm, but mild requests for a whole roof or plumbing repairs were pigeonholed with her sharecroppers' pleas for safely covered wells and weatherproof barns. We did, however, get treated to some porch shingles after we sat her under the worst leak during a summer thunderstorm. The need of a new, important bathroom fixture was harder to demonstrate so she merely continued to point out that, functioning or not, it was at least porcelain and inside the house, frequently following this happy thought by the remark that the floors certainly looked dreadful (all too true!) and why didn't *we* do them over!

What our neighbors thought of us we never discovered and perhaps it was just as well, for while all proper grandmothers rocked on their porches in starched house dresses, spring found me clad in earth-covered slacks getting rid of a waistline by helping plow. Summer not only saw us drinking iced white wine instead of beer, but dining at the unchristian hour of eight; and in fall and winter I took long walks when, of course, I should have been frantically fighting the black dust with which our four coal stoves so generously coated the furniture and woodwork.

Most memories are happier for we soon discovered friends who agreed that seven in the evening was the time to be sharing a congenial cocktail rather than drying the dinner dishes. The crossroad store suffered few wartime shortages, and even though its kindly proprietor had never heard of "fancy French things like lentils" he was almost the only tradesperson who didn't regard us suspiciously as "new people," and he played no favorites.

A surly steer fattened in the meadow, facing a patriotic though unmourned death to provide us with meat, and our small plot bore lavishly in spite of its scornful neighborhood title of "the book garden." Best of all, in May and June, the edges of the fields were thick with spears of wild asparagus. For weeks we ate our fill, gladly suffering the loss of local prestige that followed its picking. Our favorite was simple BUTTERED ASPARAGUS. Scrape the asparagus, remove the tough ends, and tie the stalks into easily handled small bunches, with 2-inch wide strips of cloth. Cover with boiling salted water and cook until just tender. Drain, remove the strips of cloth, and serve the asparagus on triangles of crisp buttered toast with a little more melted butter over the tips.

Sometimes the butter has a bruised garlic clove added to it as it melts. The garlic is removed and 1 tablespoon of bread crumbs browned in each ½ cup of the butter for ITALIAN ASPARAGUS, and 1 teaspoon of grated Parmesan cheese on each serving doesn't seem to change the name but gives a very different delicious flavor. Hollandaise sauce (page 97) can have its day, too, as a cover; white sauce (page 94) and cheese sauce (page 95) each come in for a welcome and when a filling course for lunch seems indicated we have COUNTRY ASPARAGUS. Prepare the asparagus as in the first recipe, serve it on toast with butter, and accompany each helping with a freshly boiled, shelled 10-minute egg. This gets mashed into the hot green tips as they are eaten and it's a dish for the gods.

ASPARAGUS SOUFFLÉ. Beat the yolks of 4 eggs until light, add to 1 cup of white sauce (page 94), and beat until well mixed. Add 1 cup of chopped cooked asparagus tips, a scrape of onion or 1 teaspoon of minced chives. Add salt and pepper if necessary and fold in the stiffly beaten whites of 4 eggs. Pour into a buttered baking dish. Place the dish in a shallow pan of water and bake at 350° for 45 minutes. This is a most delicate and delicious main course for luncheon. If desired, the egg yolks, asparagus, and white sauce can be mixed ahead and the beaten egg whites added just before baking.

Later in the summer, our own broccoli and cauliflower were cooked just as the asparagus and varied with the same sauces, but before that time we had all the ripe tomatoes and golden bantam corn we could hold.

Have you ever tried FRESH TOMATO JUICE for breakfast? Simmer 1 quart of ripe quartered tomatoes with 1 teaspoon of chopped onion and an optional tiny bit of garlic and a leaf or so of basil, until the juice just starts to flow. Press gently through a sieve, add salt and a grind of black pepper, and chill overnight. Next morning stir, before serving in glasses floating a slight dust of celery salt and a thin slice of lemon. Worcestershire sauce and tabasco can be on the table, too, but why ruin the lovely garden flavor?

STEWED TOMATOES should never be thickened with bread crumbs, flour, or, perish the thought, cornstarch, but simmered uncovered until just the right consistency. This may take from 1 to 3 hours, depending on the juiciness of the vegetable. Peel 3 times the quantity of tomatoes you will finally need and cut in quarters, so to serve four to six people start with 12 or 14 cups of tomatoes. Add 2 teaspoons of chopped onion and 1 tablespoon of salt, and ⅛ teaspoon of black pepper and let simmer as directed. Half an hour before serving add a leaf of sweet basil or a pinch of the same herb if you have it. Accompany the tomatoes with big baked sweet potatoes, and fresh corn on the cob and who cares whether meat is on the menu!

STUFFED TOMATOES. Remove 1½ or 2 tablespoons of the flesh from the tops of medium-sized ripe tomatoes. Do not hollow them completely as advised in so many recipes. After all you're going to eat tomatoes, not bread crumbs. Salt the insides slightly and place in a greased shallow baking dish. For each 4 tomatoes, soften 1 teaspoon of chopped onion in 2 tablespoons of cooking oil or butter. Remove from the fire, add 1 cup of coarse dry bread crumbs, ½ teaspoon of salt, a dash of pepper, and a pinch of thyme. Perhaps a bit of dried or fresh sweet basil can go in, too. Moisten with the juice from the removed portions of tomatoes squeezed through a sieve or your fingers. The mixture should be barely damp and never doughy. Pack the stuffing lightly into the tomatoes, heap what is left on top, and cover each one with a 1-inch square of bacon. Bake in a 375° oven for 30 minutes or until the tomatoes are just soft and the bacon crisp and brown.

SCALLOPED TOMATOES for four or six. Peel 6 or 8 tomatoes, place them loosely in a deep, greased baking dish, and surround and cover with 2 cups of the stuffing in the recipe for stuffed tomatoes (above), to which has been added ½ teaspoon of sugar. Dot the crumbs with butter and bake 45 minutes at 375°.

FRIED TOMATOES WITH CREAM GRAVY contradict the tradition of never serving two dishes cooked alike at one meal, for they are perfect with fried fish. Remove the stem and blossom from firm tomatoes and cut in thick—about ¾ inch-slices. Add 1 teaspoon of salt and ½ teaspoon of black pepper to 1 cup of flour, place on a paper plate or waxed paper, and coat the cut slices of the tomatoes thoroughly. Heat ½ inch of grease—bacon fat is far and away the best—until just smoking, using an iron skillet that will not crowd the tomatoes. Gently slide in the slices and cook over a medium hot fire until each side is deep brown, turning the tomato only once. This should take some 10 minutes for each side. Place the tomatoes on a platter and keep hot. For the 10 or 12 slices that will serve four or six add 1½ tablespoons of the seasoned flour to the juices remaining in the pan, blend, scraping up all the delicate essence from the bottom, then slowly add 2 cups of rich milk. Cook 10 minutes, stirring occasionally, then pour over the tomatoes. A pinch of sweet basil may be added to the gravy and a garnish of crisp bacon to the finished dish. Big baked potatoes again, and a green salad with this make a most satisfying lunch.

FRIED GREEN TOMATOES are so good that we for one family often sacrificed the unripened vegetables. Cook them just as in the above recipe and make their gravy in the same pan too, with thick sour cream and 2 teaspoons of flour. A gourmet's dream.

In the summers when Diamond Jim Brady drove a spanking pair around New Jersey's Atlantic Highlands, with Lillian Russell lolling in full-blown beauty beside him, he was the constant patron of a small inn hidden away in a nearby deserted village. Although his business ethics may have been open to question, Diamond Jim admittedly knew his vittles, and he spread the fame of the inn's boiled corn on the cob so widely that ere long the once rustic bungalow became a large restaurant, flourishing until Prohibition forced its closing. But before the French proprietor died—of a broken heart they said—he told me the simple way he prepared the dish that had brought him fame and fortune.

BOILED CORN À LA DELISLE. Carefully remove the silk from fresh corn but leave on enough of the green husk to cover each ear. Have ready a large kettle of boiling milk and water, half-and-half. Cook the corn in this— keeping it well covered with the liquid—for 5 or 10 minutes depending on its age, then drain it thoroughly and serve it wrapped in a napkin. Allow each diner to husk his own and you're in for a happy surprise with the first delicious bite. Not to mention that corn cooked in this fashion seems to need a surprisingly small amount of butter.

Tender corn on the cob admittedly can never be improved upon but when the kernels toughen or grandfather and his sore teeth come for a meal, serve CREAMED CORN. Score the raw kernels and scrape from the cob.

Add to each cup 2 tablespoons of cream, ½ teaspoon of salt, ¼ teaspoon of pepper, and 1 teaspoon of butter. Place in a double boiler, cover, and cook over boiling water for 15 minutes. 1 tablespoon of chopped sautéed green or red pepper added to this makes CORN MEXICAINE.

Grandfather, or anyone else for that matter, will love CORN OYSTERS. Prepare the corn as above, add ½ cup of rich milk, 2 tablespoons of flour, a shake of salt, pepper, 1 teaspoon of melted butter, and 1 beaten egg to each cupful. Cook the batter by the teaspoonful on a lightly greased hot griddle. They should be thin and delicate.

CORN FRITTERS are heartier and can make use of leftovers. For four or six, cut 2 cups of cooked corn from the cob, add ½ cup of sifted flour, ½ teaspoon of salt, a shake of pepper, and the yolks of 3 eggs. Beat well, then fold in 3 stiffly beaten egg whites. Fry in 1-inch deep, hot cooking fat. Brown both sides and serve immediately. These are the thing to go with stewed chicken.

CORN LOUISIANA for four or six. Pare and quarter lengthwise 3 big sweet potatoes. Boil in salted water until just tender, which takes between 10 and 15 minutes. Drain. Dip one end of each piece in sherry and then in brown sugar. Place around the edge of a greased baking dish, sugared ends up. Pour in the center 2 cups of corn Mexicaine (page 88). Dot the corn with 1 teaspoon of butter and dust lightly with fine bread crumbs. Bake in a 400° oven for 15 or 20 minutes until the potatoes just start to brown. This is the perfect partner for baked ham.

BAKED SQUASH. Wash and remove the stem ends from tender young yellow squash. Cut in small dice, not removing the seeds unless they are very coarse. For four or six, put 3 cups of the diced vegetable in a greased baking dish, add ½ cup of water, ½ teaspoon of salt, ⅛ teaspoon of pepper, 2 tablespoons of butter, and 1 teaspoon of scraped onion. Cover closely and bake at 375° for 20 minutes or until the squash is tender.

Everyone knows that cucumbers are the correct accompaniment for fish but most cooks are content to serve thin slivers in French dressing, forgetting that the grown pickle was once considered a vegetable as well as a salad. Few today know that it combines beautifully with the lowly spinach. Both the following recipes call for cooked spinach, chopped or put through the meat grinder. Again let your motto be "Do it ahead," or use leftovers. STUFFED CUCUMBERS for four or six. Scrub 4 medium-sized cucumbers, trim the stem ends, cut in half lengthwise and remove the seeds. Boil the boat-shaped pieces for 5 minutes in salted water. Drain thoroughly. Add ½ cup of white sauce (page 94) to 2 cups of chopped spinach. Season with salt, pepper, and a tiny scrape of onion, heap it in the cucumber boats, dust the top with bread crumbs, a few bits of butter and just the ghost of

grated Parmesan cheese. Place in a greased shallow dish and bake for 10 or 15 minutes in a 400° oven until the crumbs are brown. Serve immediately.

SPINACH RING WITH CUCUMBERS. Pack a greased ring mould with 4 cups of chopped spinach that has been seasoned with salt, pepper, a few grains of cayenne, and a bit of onion. Set the mould in a shallow pan of water and place in a 325° oven about 25 minutes to become thoroughly heated. Peel and slice thinly 3 cups of cucumbers. Boil for 5 minutes in salted water and drain thoroughly. Turn the spinach from the mould on to a hot platter, fill the center with the cucumbers, and cover with hollandaise sauce (page 97). This is delicious, looks elaborate, and is really easy, for the spinach and the cucumbers can be kept hot and the sauce doesn't mind a little delay either.

This recipe for BAKED EGGPLANT was a lifesaver in the days of meat rationing. Cut 1 medium-sized eggplant in half, cover with salted water, and boil 5 minutes. Drain, peel, and cut into 1-inch dice. Boil 1 cup of rice 5 minutes in salted water, drain, and add to the eggplant. Soften 1 cup of sliced onions and 1 minced clove of garlic in 2 tablespoons of butter or cooking oil. Add 2½ cups of canned or fresh peeled chopped tomatoes to the eggplant and rice, mix lightly, add 1 teaspoon of salt, and ⅛ teaspoon of pepper, and put in a greased baking dish. Dust the top with ½ cup of bread crumbs and an optional teaspoon of Parmesan cheese, add a few bits of butter, and bake for 45 minutes at 350°. If it seems dry when not quite done, gently add a little tomato juice or diluted consommé so as not to disturb the top. The finished dish should not be runny, and the tomatoes, eggplant and rice each distinct and separate.

Our first country winter shut down on two city-slickers, ignorant till then that a dearth of fresh vegetables must come with the frost. I had done no canning and the distance of forty miles to the nearest big city market might as well have been four hundred to the possessors of an "A" gas ticket. Both vitamins and variety had to be supplied by the local store's constant but uninspiring cabbage, celery, and carrots. The only remaining question was how to prepare that ever-present trio appetizingly.

Turning away from the usual long cooking, and accompanying smell, I found CABBAGE delectable if first thinly sliced as for cole slaw, crisped for ½ hour in ice water, and then plunged into rapidly boiling salted water for 5 or not more than 10 minutes. Drain it well—2½ cups will serve four or six—and cover, not mix, the hot slivers with white sauce (page 94) or cheese sauce (page 95) for a surprisingly good everyday green. For special occasions blanket it with hollandaise sauce (page 97) and you'll find it's a dish fit to grace a banquet.

Not at all delicate and only to be attempted in a well-ventilated kitchen is SMOTHERED CABBAGE. Chop, wash, and drain 10 cups of cabbage. Melt ½ cup of bacon, ham or pork fat in a skillet, add the cabbage, cover, and cook over a medium fire for 30 minutes, stirring occasionally, until the cabbage is soft and reduced to half its original bulk. Remove the cover, increase the heat, and continue cooking and stirring until the cabbage starts to brown—15 minutes or a little longer. This is a good lusty Negro dish and undoubtedly the one on which Topsy "just growed," for its odor alone ought to increase a midget's height. But try it with broiled ham and see if it doesn't stick to the ribs.

CELERY, too, turned out surprisingly delicious, and glamorous to boot, when I ceased cutting the stalks in dice but instead left each bunch whole, trimmed the root, sheared off the tops well down (save them for soups and garnishes) and then split each bunch lengthwise, root and all, into quarters or sixths, depending on its size. Scrape the outside of the stalks if necessary and cook in as little water as possible. Save the water to add to the morning tomato juice.

BRAISED CELERY. Boil the celery about 5 or 8 minutes in salted water until not quite tender. Drain, return to the stove, and add ½ cup of canned consommé or stock and 1 tablespoon of butter. Cover and let steam about 5 minutes longer, until the celery is done, then remove the lid and cook over a hot fire until the juice is reduced one half. Serve immediately. Drained, chilled and covered with French dressing this is CELERY EN BRANCHE and guess what vinaigrette dressing makes it—CELERY VINAIGRETTE.

CREOLE CELERY. Boil celery in salted water 10 minutes, drain and cover with creole sauce (page 95).

For CELERY AU GRATIN we'll have to go back to first principles and slice the stalks crosswise in 1-inch lengths. 2 cupfuls will serve four or six. Boil the celery in salted water until tender, drain, and mix with 2½ cups of white sauce (page 94) and ½ cup of grated cheese. Cover with bread crumbs, dot with butter, and bake in a greased dish at 400° for 20 minutes or until the crumbs are brown.

Four months of constant struggle with carrots still left me cold to their possibilities except for roasting them whole around lamb or beef, although my BRAISED WHOLE CARROTS, first scraped and then cooked like braised celery, have been pronounced delicious, as have MINTED CARROTS. For four or six, scrape and cut 2 cups of carrots into eighths—about the size of big matches. Boil 5 minutes in salted water. Drain. Return to the fire and add 1 tablespoon of butter and 1 tablespoon of mint jelly. Stir over a medium hot fire until the jelly melts, and serve.

Even the thought of these last two recipes is followed by none of the pangs of hunger or mouthwatering anticipation that has come with writing the directions for cooking the other vegetables, so just let's say, "carrots can be cooked and eaten, but why?" and leave them to those nursery pals and garden scourges, Flopsy, Mopsy, Cottontail and Peter.

It's a Cinch with Sauces

How many little girls today read Louisa M. Alcott, I wonder? Compared to comic books and Western movies her old-fashioned stories must seem lacking in action, yet once the four March sisters were as real to me as Orphan Annie to the present generation.

What I felt was "offensively" good health—I still can't even look delicate—kept me from following poor Beth's example and seeking an early grave. The less spiritual ambition of owning a toy cookstove that really worked, such as Daisy had in *Little Men*, was more easily achieved and from the morning I saw it under the Christmas tree I've never regretted the choice I was forced to make. Just as well, too, for health and a cookstove still continue to keep me from any higher plane.

My toy stove was a square tin box, had a smoke pipe and two cooking holes and was completely outfitted with doll-size pots and pans. The heat came from a metal tube out of which sprouted two candle-shaped objects stuffed with cotton, and when alcohol was poured on and a match applied, a hot but, as I learnt, completely unadjustable flame was the result.

My mother, who was no cook but, like every good housewife in those days, knew "how things should be done," appeared in the nursery as soon as my new toy was set up, announcing that she was going to teach me one worthwhile thing before I started to mess. This turned out to be white sauce and worthwhile it is—and how few cooks still understand its manufacture, as witness the paste that so often masquerades under that name in restaurants or, even sadder, on the home table. Her recipe for WHITE SAUCE remains the right and only one. Melt 2 tablespoons of butter over a medium flame and stir in 2 tablespoons of flour. When things start to bubble take the pan from the fire and stir in 1 cup of milk. Do this very slowly; let the flour absorb the liquid and not a lump remain. Put the pan back over the heat and just as slowly add 1 cup more of milk, never ceasing the constant stirring. Add 1 teaspoon of salt and ⅛ teaspoon of black pepper, and keep it over a lower heat for at least 10 min-utes longer, stirring occasionally. If you must neglect it after the last milk goes in, put the sauce into the top of a double boiler to finish cooking over hot water. This makes a medium thin sauce which can be thickened by a tablespoon more of flour and butter added before the milk, or by adding flour diluted to a thin paste with milk after the sauce first starts to thicken. But beware of a floury taste in the finished sauce and always cook it thoroughly.

I regret to say that the toy stove was wrenched from me shortly after this lesson, for after one afternoon alone in its company I was discovered trying to camouflage a badly singed pair of eyebrows with a lead pencil and preferred not to discuss a suspicious scorch on the nursery ceiling. Mother's recipe was the first I taught my daughter after the young man appeared who turned her thoughts to things culinary, but behind locked lips has lain till this day how I acquired intimate knowledge of the dire results that follow pouring alcohol on a lighted wick.

The method of making this foundation sauce should be practiced patiently until you are sure of your technique for, though good alone, it is the base of numerous others. Below are just a few suggestions.

To make CHEESE SAUCE leave the white sauce in the double boiler and stir in ½ cup or more of grated sharp cheese until the cheese has melted and the desired flavor is obtained.

IMITATION SAUCE NEWBURG. Dilute 2 beaten egg yolks with ½ cup of milk, pour 2 cups of hot white sauce over them, and return to the double boiler and stir for 5 minutes. Before serving add 1 tablespoon of sherry.

MUSHROOM SAUCE. Sauté 1 cup of chopped mushrooms in the butter and proceed as in plain white sauce.

EGG SAUCE. Add 2 chopped hard-boiled eggs to the white sauce just before serving.

CELERY SAUCE calls for 1 cup of the sieved cooked vegetable, 1 cup of the water in which it was cooked, and 1 cup of milk. Proceed as in white sauce.

Make ONION SAUCE the same way.

CAPER SAUCE NUMBER 1 as on page 78.

CAPER SAUCE NUMBER 2. Add ½ cup of capers to white sauce.

CAPER SAUCE NUMBER 3. Boil 2½ cups of chicken broth (made with bouillon cubes if necessary) until reduced to 2 cups. Melt 2 tablespoons each of flour and butter as in white sauce. Add broth slowly and 3 tablespoons each of capers and their liquor. Cook until thickened and before serving stir in 2 tablespoons of sour cream. Any caper sauce is good on fish.

CREOLE SAUCE. Soften ½ cup of chopped peeled onion, ½ cup of chopped green pepper, and half a chopped garlic clove in 2 tablespoons of butter. Add 3½ cups of peeled chopped or canned tomatoes. Simmer ½ hour. Thicken by rubbing 2 tablespoons of flour into 2 tablespoons of butter. Dilute this with ½ cup of the sauce and return to the sauce, stirring until well mixed and simmering 10 minutes longer. Watery tomatoes may need a little more thickening. This sauce is fine on cooked shrimps, fish, or meat, disguises leftovers, and will even make boiled tripe taste less like bath towels.

REAL SAUCE NEWBURG. Scald 2 cups of thin cream in the top of a double boiler. Beat the yolks of 3 eggs until light with 1 teaspoon of salt and a few grains of cayenne. Slowly stir into them the scalded cream. Cook in the boiler over a low heat until just thick and before serving add 2 tablespoons of sherry. This can have in it ½ cup of sautéed chopped mushrooms and the same amount of pimento or sautéed green peppers, and is perhaps the most difficult sauce to make. Take it from over the hot water as soon as thickened, add the cooked lobster, shrimps, scallops or what have you, cut in large pieces, and return over the hot water until well heated through but not a minute longer. It must never be boiled.

Preparing really good GRAVY takes just as much patience and practice as white sauce. Remove the cooked meat from its roasting pan and keep it warm. Leave about 2 tablespoons of fat in the pan and place it over a medium heat. Stir in 1½ tablespoons of flour and while doing so scrape up every bit of the meaty residue from the bottom of the pan. Slowly stir in 2 cups of water, 1 teaspoon of salt and ⅛ teaspoon of pepper. Let simmer, stirring occasionally, for 10 minutes. This is another foundation recipe and is fun to experiment with. Change its flavor with a little chopped onion or mushrooms, and try out tomato juice or red wine and meat sauces such as Worcestershire in it, too. Instead of using plain water experiment with canned consommé, diluted ½ with water. This makes a very flavorful gravy, and see what a delightful difference the addition of a few tablespoons of sour cream makes.

RED WINE GRAVY. Soften 1 tablespoon of chopped onion or, better, chives, in 2 tablespoons of butter. Blend in 1½ tablespoons of flour, then stir in, slowly, 1 cup of red wine and 1 cup of canned consommé, or stock. Add 1 teaspoon of chopped parsley, stir and simmer for 10 minutes. This is good with any leftover red meat.

WHITE WINE GRAVY is made the same way with ½ white wine and ½ chicken broth for the liquid, and goes with cooked chicken, veal, or pork. Either wine gravy takes to a few chopped celery leaves or a grating of raw carrot; and 1 teaspoon of dry or French mustard added before the final simmering makes it just right for smoked ham or tongue.

SWEET SOUR SAUCE is either red or white wine gravy (above) with 1 tablespoon of vinegar, 2 tablespoons of raisins, and 1 teaspoon of sugar added, and simmered for a few minutes before serving over the meat of your choice.

The HORSERADISH SAUCE that is so necessary on boiled or roast beef is simply 2 cups of thick sour cream mixed with bottled horseradish to taste.

LEMON BUTTER belongs with simpler sauces, too, for its ingredients are those in its title: 2 tablespoons or more of strained lemon juice added to ½ cup of melted butter. This goes well on green vegetables and with the addition of a little minced parsley or chives is fine on broiled, baked or fried fish.

Perhaps because its complicated directions in her kitchen cookbook were such a test of temperament as well as of culinary ability, Mother always demanded a knowledge of hollandaise sauce, before she engaged a new cook. My own family loves the sauce, too, but as my cooks needed most the easygoing nature that allowed them to reset the table for unexpected guests and then wait placidly while we downed an extra unhurried cocktail, I devised a recipe for hollandaise that had the same traits as its cooks and was as near foolproof as possible. When you master its simple directions, it will appear frequently on your table. So, if you can buy a small double boiler— one that an egg beater will just fit into without banging the sides—for its making, then without a worry learn the answer to Mother's $64-question.

Dependable HOLLANDAISE SAUCE. Melt ¾ to 1 cup of butter in the top of a double boiler. Add 2 tablespoons of strained lemon juice. Beat 3 egg yolks light with ½ teaspoon of salt and a few grains of cayenne. Slowly beat into them the melted butter and juice. Be sure the hot water does not touch the bottom of the inset, then return the eggs and butter to the boiler, add 3 tablespoons of hot water and beat constantly over a low heat until the sauce just starts to thicken. Judge this crucial stage by the slight creases that will appear in its erstwhile youthful countenance, and when reached, remove the sauce from over the hot water immediately, for it's done. You, too, are having that extra cocktail, or the head of the house has decided a scrub-up and fresh shirt are what he needs just as dinner is announced? The sauce will keep perfectly, smooth and uncurdled, although perhaps not quite so light, for 15 or 20 minutes. Fill the bottom of the double boiler with lukewarm water and place the sauce, covered, over it. Console yourself with the remembrance that even in the best hotels, hollandaise is never served steaming and concentrate on the simpler task of keeping really hot what the sauce is to go on.

BÉARNAISE SAUCE uses 3 tablespoons of tarragon vinegar instead of the lemon juice, and is made and kept hot just as hollandaise.

Old cookbooks recommend olive oil as a base for both these sauces instead of butter. It is quite as good, and cooking oil is also acceptable in a pinch. But never, never experiment here with vegetable shortening. Desperation drove me to this once, but like the blaze in the nursery, don't let's discuss it.

Salad Days and Ways for Dressing Them

My artist-uncle spent the greatest part of his Bohemian existence in France, returning to his native city for rare but eagerly awaited visits, perhaps to do a family portrait but most certainly to tell the world, with gestures, how much better everything was arranged "over there."

When my turn came to be transferred to canvas I sat motionless by the hour, afraid to break the spell of his youthful and delightfully bawdy memories of Quatz' Arts balls and Parisian life in the late 1890s. Visiting him there later, the studio of his more settled years turned out to be just a large untidy loft, disappointingly empty of beautiful undraped women, but a thrilling spot to eat lunch. I trotted excitedly beside Uncle Charlie while he bargained in slangy French for more varieties of lettuce and greens than I'd ever known existed, carried the yard-long still warm bread and pat of sweet butter, and helped choose the ripe cheese and light pastries. Then, as tea brewed over whistling gas, I set the model's throne with peasant pottery and steel knives and forks, while he made the salad, and after its first taste no longer wondered at the picturesque epithets that had garnished his demands for real olive oil, a pepper grinder and wine vinegar back in my own home. Although his measurements for dressing were strictly rule of thumb, he was firm that the only way to get the correct whisper of garlic was to rub a cut clove of it over a small piece of dry crust or toast and then break the bread into bits in the salad bowl. Heavy Spanish olive oil was his preference and he produced his own WINE VINEGAR by leaving an opened bottle of red or white wine to sour on a sunny window sill, recorking it after it became tart enough to please him, and my neat soul was at first outraged by his casual wipe of the unwashed wooden bowl after we had finished our salad.

With these hints, get out a salad bowl with its fork and spoon and start an artistic career of your own. Experiment with combinations of lettuces and herbs, and equip a tray with different brands and bottles of oil and flavored vinegar, not forgetting a castor of assorted salts and a pepper grinder. Olive oil must be bought, but FLAVORED VINEGAR can be made in your own kitchen with no more effort than was expended by Uncle Charlie, a notoriously lazy creature. Pour heated wine or cider vinegar over contents of a jar previously loosely filled with the bruised fresh herb of your choice, leaving it tightly sealed for 10 days or until the desired flavor is achieved. Then strain. Two or three tablespoons of dried herbs per quart of vinegar will have the same result. Tarragon is the classic for this but you'll soon want to go on to basil, celery, lemon, thyme and nasturtium. Not only explore the shops but the roadside for fillings for your bowl and you'll find that peppery cress, sour grass, or wild sorrel, and that curse of a smooth lawn, the dandelion's leaves, add to its flavor and texture. Before you realize, you'll have your own determined opinion on the correct measurements and ingredients of a delicious individual FRENCH DRESSING, but good beginning proportions are ¼ cup of vinegar, ½ teaspoon of dry mustard, 1 teaspoon of salt, ⅛ teaspoon of pepper, 1 teaspoon of paprika, mixed with ¾ cup of olive oil. Add a tablespoon of tomato catsup and/or a bit of grated onion once in a while as a welcome surprise, and for a real change make SOUR CREAM DRESSING with ¾ cup of sour cream in place of the olive oil. This is particularly good over sliced cucumbers flecked with the green of minced chives.

CREOLE DRESSING is best made beforehand and is the perfect teammate for the beautiful gold and white Belgian endive. Add ½ cup each of tomato catsup and finely chopped watercress to 1 cup of french dressing (above).

ROQUEFORT DRESSING needs ⅛ pound of the cheese, at least, added to 1 cup of French dressing (above), and CHEDDAR DRESSING—made in the same proportions—calls for that cheese to be well aged.

A quick VINAIGRETTE DRESSING is ½ cup of the red tomato pickle (page 128) added to 1 cup of French dressing (above).

A more elaborate VINAIGRETTE DRESSING NUMBER 2 is ⅛ cup of tarragon vinegar, ½ cup of cider or wine vinegar, 1 teaspoon of dry mustard, 2 tablespoons of chopped chives, ½ teaspoon of finely chopped onion, ½ cup of chopped peeled tomato, 1 tablespoon of chopped celery and the same of green pepper. Add salt, pepper, paprika, and a few grains of cayenne, and mix everything well with ½ cup of olive oil. Either of these two are delicious on asparagus and give a useful tang to a salad made of cold cooked string beans.

My father loved any salad and was so fond of raw tomatoes that he ate them for breakfast in an age where still lingered a trace of the old fear of the red "love apples." Many a time have I seen him make his summer lunch a big ice-cold dish of thinly sliced tomatoes and Bermuda onion rings, literally mopping the saucer with a thick crust of bread to get up any French dressing that had escaped. He liked cucumbers and celery in this, too, and long before our vitamin-conscious age, maintained that cucumbers were best without the usual preliminary soaking in ice water, but chilled and sliced paper thin unskinned. Modern dietitians would also approve of the simple and delicious CELERY COLE SLAW that he always demanded with any fowl. For four or six, add 2 teaspoons of ground dry mustard to 1 cup of French dressing (page 100) and pour it over 3 cups of diced crisp celery. Serve it well chilled in saucers as Father liked it, and watch the dunking.

His cole slaw never was touched with mayonnaise but must always have over it my grandmother's BOILED DRESSING. Beat together ¾ cup of cider vinegar, ¾ cup of rich milk, the yolks of 2 eggs, 1 teaspoon each of dry mustard and salt, and 1 tablespoon of sugar. Cook in the top of a double boiler over boiling water until it starts to thicken, stirring constantly. Add the beaten whites of 2 eggs and 2 tablespoons of cooking oil, remove from the fire and beat until well mixed.

BOILED DRESSING NUMBER 2 is just as old a recipe, good, too, and perhaps a little easier. Bring to a boil 6 tablespoons of butter or cooking oil, 6 tablespoons of sweet or sour cream, 1 teaspoon each of salt and dry mustard, 2 teaspoons of sugar, and ¾ cup of cider vinegar. Remove from the fire and stir slowly over 3 whole eggs that have been beaten until frothy. Return to a double boiler and beat hard over hot water until just thick—about 5 minutes.

Both of these recipes for dressing should be cooled a little before pouring over the 4 cups of shredded cabbage that will make COLE SLAW for four or six. 1 cup of coarsely grated carrots will add an up-to-date color and flavor to the cabbage, but for a real old-time taste and appearance stir in 2 tablespoons of celery seed after mixing the cole slaw.

Boiled dressing is good, too, on tomatoes or plain lettuce, but to still the occasional yearning for MAYONNAISE make it easily and quickly this way! Beat the yolks of 2 eggs, 2 tablespoons of lemon juice or vinegar, 1 teaspoon each of salt and dry mustard, and a few grains of cayenne in a chilled bowl. Add 2 cups of olive oil or salad oil, starting to drip it in slowly and stirring constantly. This is a basic recipe—add more lemon juice or mustard to your own taste or perhaps a cup of sour cream after the dressing is made.

RUSSIAN DRESSING is mayonnaise (above) or boiled dressing (above) added to an equal amount of chili sauce or tomato catsup, and improves the sometimes dull flavor of winter iceberg lettuce.

The sticky heaps of jellied marshmallows and tinted fruit that appear on too many tables should be shudderingly avoided along with their sickeningly sweet mayonnaise but my POTATO SALAD is something quite different. Chop 4 slices of bacon, brown, and reserve the grease. Drain the bacon and mix with 3 cups of diced cold boiled potatoes. Heat 3 tablespoons of the bacon grease, add 4 tablespoons of chopped chives—or 1 tablespoon of chopped onion—1 tablespoon of parsley, an optional tablespoon of chopped fresh dill, 1 teaspoon of salt, ¼ teaspoon of black pepper, and ½ cup of vinegar. Pour this while still hot over the potatoes, cover and chill them, overnight if you wish, and when ready to serve mix ½ cup of mayonnaise with the potatoes and serve on lettuce garnished with more mayonnaise and perhaps stuffed or sliced hard-boiled eggs, quartered tomatoes, and olives. This, of course, is the perfect companion for slices of cold smoked ham and dill pickles.

For an equally good salad with cold pork, veal, or chicken, serve WALDORF SALAD. Make this of 2 cups of diced very sour apples with an equal quantity of chopped celery mixed with 2 cups of tart mayonnaise. Add ½ cup of broken nut meats before serving on lettuce and trim with whole halves of nuts.

A ring of tomato jelly filled with celery or cabbage cole slaw looks and tastes delicious. A quick method for the jelly is on page 161, but when time is no object make TOMATO JELLY NUMBER 2. Chop ¼ cup of onions and ½ small clove of garlic. Add to 3½ cups of tomato juice or 4 cups of canned or peeled chopped whole ones. Bring to a boil, add 1 small piece of bay leaf, 1 clove and a few peppercorns, 1 teaspoon of salt, and a few grains of cayenne. Simmer for 20 or 30 minutes, strain, and thoroughly dissolve in the hot liquid 2 tablespoons of gelatine. Pour into a very lightly greased mould. Chill and place in the refrigerator 2 or 3 hours until firm.

My débutante activities weren't distinguished by the hectic rush that follows the modern "coming out." Teas then were attended mostly by white-gloved ancients whose approval of the bud's behavior really mattered, and having a well-filled dance card and—oh, joy!—"splitting your waltzes" were the height of popularity. Hearty food was served at even the smallest, most informal affair. When I read of the simple scrambled-egg-and-sausage suppers at balls today, my mind goes back to plates heaped with scalloped oysters, Virginia ham, and chicken salad.

Last winter an elderly, crotchety cousin decided to celebrate his birthday with a family party. The abrupt invitation on the phone was typically cheerless: "I'll be seventy on Saturday. Probably my last birthday. Thought I'd give a supper with decent food. Chicken salad and oysters. Don't come if you don't like 'em!"

The menu he promised was certainly nostalgic and more than a little lacking in vitamins, but so many of his guests enjoyed second and even third helpings, that by the end of the evening not a single family argument had taken place and Cousin Joseph himself was in a better humor than any of us ever remembered.

Here is how he had ordered the CHICKEN SALAD made. For four or six: Cover a 5-pound (or a little less) cut-up stewing chicken with water, add 1 small sliced onion, a sprig of parsley and ½ cup of chopped celery leaves. Bring to a boil and simmer until the bird is tender, adding 1 tablespoon of salt when half done and allowing the meat to cool in the water in which it was cooked. Drain the chicken thoroughly and cut it into 1-inch dice. Once more no modern "mincing" please, and be sure to remove every bit of skin and gristle. There should be about 3¼ cups of the meat. Chop 1¼ cups of tender inside stalks of celery, add ½ teaspoon of salt and toss it lightly with the cut-up chicken before putting it in the refrigerator to become thoroughly chilled. Mix 1 cup of mayonnaise (page 102) with an equal amount of boiled dressing (page 102), and mix half of this with the chicken and celery. When ready to serve, turn this out on an ice-cold platter that has first been lined with crisp lettuce and pour over it the balance of the dressing. Decorate the platter with 3 sliced hard-boiled eggs and ½ cup of sliced stuffed olives. Scatter an optional ¼ cup of capers over all.

CRAB SALAD is made the same way using 1 pound of cooked crab meat instead of the chicken; and TOMATO SURPRISE is a hollowed tomato resting on a few frilly leaves of lettuce and filled with either chicken or crab salad. Just who is "surprised" by this I've never understood, certainly not the diners, but it's a grand start for a summer lunch, as is AVOCADO SURPRISE with the halved and seeded pear filled with crab salad.

One "broke," but enjoyable, summer we shared a cottage with friends whose children were the same age as our own, and July and August resembled a continuous college house party. The number of guests present was always doubtful until the last late breakfaster had repaired to the beach and even then I was never sure how many more would drift back to raid the icebox at lunchtime. Fortunately a handy boardwalk hot-dog stand took some of the edge off their youthful appetites, but salad, sandwiches, and milk always seemed to be in demand about two o'clock. I had forgotten the most enjoyed *pièce de résistance* until I recently encountered that summer's permanent guest, now a sedate (or so he thinks) married stockbroker. He greeted me with, "Would you please tell my wife how you made that good Slop Salad, she says she has never heard of it." Hardly to be wondered at either, for the name given it by its enthusiastic eaters doesn't sound very inviting, and probably SALAD À LA RUSSE would appeal much more. Call it what you will, this is it: For four or six, take 3 cups of cooked string beans, 1 cup of skinned chopped tomatoes, ½ cup of chopped celery, and 1 Bermuda onion cut in thin rings. Add 1 cup, or a little more if you have it, of diced cooked meat or fish and toss everything together in a big bowl with 1 cup of shredded lettuce and 2 cups of French dressing (page 100). Not a difficult recipe, is it, and needless to say its ingredients can be pleasantly controlled by the leftovers in your icebox. Served in deep saucers and accompanied by cheese sandwiches that my "boarders" made for themselves, it disappeared by the gallon and I could watch the crowd take off for their afternoon soaking secure in the knowledge that my houseful had had a filling, balanced meal.

Of course the type of salad that is to be served at any meal depends mainly on the courses that are to precede or follow it, but any salad is the better for having cheese passed at the same time. Toasted crackers or warm French bread as Uncle Charlie liked it should always go along too.

The Cheese Pâté (page 206) is just as good with salad as it is as an appetizer. A well-aged bit of "rat trap" never has to be apologized for either, and this department can always stand experimental purchases in a well-stocked delicatessen, for Uncle Charlie's world of models and painters is no more interested in a new art technique than the even larger world of appreciative diners is in new touches to add to that most enjoyable of foods—*les salades*.

Mrs. Rorer's, Grandmother's and My Just Desserts

Mothers and fathers are necessary I know, but their minds are so often taken up with seeing that little Mary wears her rubbers or finishes her milk, that all children should have grandparents to give them a little extra spoiling. For nothing brings that sense of security and well-being so important to the hearts of small fry as the occasional companionship and approval of a doting elder.

In this respect I was a very lucky little girl. Not only was I my grandmother's favorite, but she lived in the country. Not on a farm in the *real* country, that would have been too much to ask, but her house in a still undeveloped suburb was a most satisfactory substitute. There was a lake surrounded with woods where I could hunt the hepatica's blue flowers in early spring; next-door neighbors kept a cow and chickens, and hay was actually mowed in a nearby field. All never-ceasing wonders to a city-bred child. There was also a tree in the backyard that produced the smallest sourest black cherries I have ever tasted. I spent many happy hours planting the fallen seeds, and such is my faith in Mother Nature that I hopefully drove by the old house just a few years ago still unable to believe that my earliest gardening experiment was a complete failure.

But the kitchen is where my memory really lingers, for in it Grandmother spent most of her time, always willing to let me help by licking the yellow bowl clean of its remaining cake batter or drying the everyday dishes. There, too, perched on a stool, I made my first acquaintance with *Mrs. Rorer's Philadelphia Cook Book* and it remains high on my list of favorite reading, although compared to today's completely standardized manuals her easy-going directions might find a more appropriate rest on the fiction shelf.

Mrs. Rorer's publishers were well ahead of their time in that they embellished their volume with a photograph of its authoress; and, while the firm common-sense face that stares from the flyleaf may lack the sex appeal of the modern female novelist, their heroines could certainly use to advantage the homely advice to cooks on proper behavior set forth in its pages.

Mrs. Rorer's list of adequate kitchen equipment covers three pages in closely printed double columns—and the recipes! Each an adventure although sometimes a depressing one, for after drooling through paragraphs on preparing boned chicken comes the stern warning that "this is almost impossible to do unless you have seen it done before" and the same discouraging advice follows puff paste. Mrs. R. may have been kindhearted in trying to keep the inexperienced cook from waste but her photograph made me feel that she was more likely to be found lurking in a cupboard ready to pop out with an "I told you so" at a failure, and I'll bet many of her less confident readers went to their graves with an unfulfilled longing for both of those delicacies.

"Game" has a long chapter to itself which gives many helps for "getting rid of the gamey flavor," and leaves the general impression that, while the little woman may have slaved away long hours at her husband's favorite bird's-nest pudding—"troublesome but beautiful when done"—in return it was a poor provider who didn't put in his dull moments at the office popping deer out of the window or, at the very least, set up a duck-blind behind his rolltop desk.

Any mention of wine is generally followed by a coy, "if you use it," although in one glorious recipe for fruitcake she cuts loose, practically thumbs her nose at the W.C.T.U., and wants on hand not only brandy and rum but demands a pint of good Champagne for soaking the finished product, ending with a nonchalant, "this well repays one for the trouble." So it may be that the lady was more tolerant than her photograph shows.

Grandmother rarely used the cookbook, which accounts for my intimacy with its contents, but when sponge cake was in the offing Mrs. Rorer was wrenched from my grasp and, repeating the still true slogan "The oven can wait for the cake, never the cake for the oven," Grandmother started on an interminable adjustment of drafts and shakings of the ancient black coalstove. Flour and sugar were each sifted five times and then balanced against selected eggs on the kitchen scales, lemon peel grated, and both my gay young aunts were conscripted to help, for though I was no hindrance to that loving heart, Grandmother was generally firm against other women being underfoot in her kitchen. Sponge cake, however, was a major undertaking. The whites and yolks of the eggs were first separated with fanatical care, placed in two big cold china platters, and each aunt received one, with a flat wire whisk and the command to keep them level and beat the contents evenly and slowly, while Grandmother dashed between, adding alternately to the platters at strategic moments the finely sifted sugar. Then the foamy masses were mixed together, the flour folded in with such care that I was almost afraid to breathe, and the precious batter was eased into its pan. Finally the oven was tested once more with Grandmother's dependable hand as a thermostat, the result of all this labor was slipped in, the door closed as gently as on a sleeping child and we were "shooed" from the kitchen for the next half-hour for fear too-unguarded footsteps or loud shouting might cause the cake to fall. If I had been especially good and quiet during these sacred rites, I was permitted to have a little of the batter which had been baked with the big cake as a "taster." The precautions always seemed most unnecessary to me, for the cake never did fall that I can remember and I felt unjustly exiled from my favorite playroom. Finally after a few tense, stealthy peeps, Grandmother announced that the cake was baked and we all trouped back to watch its golden beauty tilted from the pan, simultaneously with the disappearance of the "taster" down my hungry little throat. Grandmother split the cake in two while it was still slightly warm and spread between the pieces either tart homemade currant jelly or a creamy orange filling, but no matter what the inside held the top was never desecrated by anything more than a snowy dust of finely sifted powdered sugar. No second ring of the tea bell was needed with the delectable dessert on its way and if any pieces were left there was equal excitement at the thought of trifle or baked-cake pudding in the offing.

Grandmother's recipe, brought up to date, isn't at all troublesome—to quote my friend Mrs. Rorer—and with our dependable ovens even an inexperienced cook can easily make that pride of an old-time kitchen, and, when eggs are low in price, cheapness is added to its charms.

SPONGE CAKE. Sift flour onto waxed paper, then measure 1 cup and sift it twice more with ¼ teaspoon of salt. Sift once and measure 1 cup of sugar. Beat the whites of 5 eggs until they form peaks, then beat into them ½ cup of the sugar. Add 1 tablespoon of lemon juice and 1 tablespoon of grated lemon rind to the 5 yolks and beat until thick. Add the balance of the sugar and beat again. Combine the two egg mixtures, carefully fold in the sifted flour with an over-and-over motion, and do not beat again. Remember Grandmother's slogan and have the oven ready. Bake in one deep ungreased pan for 45 minutes at 325°, or in 2 or 3 shallower layers at 350° for 30 minutes. For CURRANT JELLY FILLING simply beat 1 cup of jelly to a spreadable consistency with a fork and put it between the small layers or the split larger cake. The ORANGE FILLING will have to be made ahead—perhaps while the cake bakes—and left to cool a little, covered, before using in the same way. Heat

1 cup of milk till scalding, in the top of a double boiler. Beat 1 tablespoon of cornstarch, the yolks of 2 eggs, and 2 tablespoons of sugar until light. Pour and stir the scalded milk slowly over them. Return to the fire, in the boiler, add 1 tablespoon of butter, and cook, stirring constantly, until just thick. Then remove from over the water and stir in 2 tablespoons of orange juice and the same amount of grated orange rind.

TRIFLE, for four or six people, has a foundation of about one third of the big sponge cake, or one whole single layer, that is two or three days old. Even a hard, stale piece will do, so keep the cake safely locked up! Put ½ cup of sherry in a shallow serving dish, follow with the cake cut in fairly thin slices, and spread with currant jelly, raspberry or strawberry jam, and let the wine absorb while making the BOILED CUSTARD. For this, scald 3 cups of milk in the top of a double boiler. Beat 3 eggs with ¼ cup of sugar and ½ teaspoon of salt. Pour and stir the hot milk over them slowly. Return to the top of the boiler, and cook over a medium fire, stirring constantly, until just thick. Remove from over the hot water immediately and stir in ¼ teaspoon of vanilla. Let cool, covered, and pour over the cake and wine. Chill before serving. Dots of more jelly or jam can decorate this and whipped cream makes a rich garnish. It is very good without the jellies, too, served as is, or with plain cream passed at the table, and altogether this famous English dessert is entirely undeserving of its boardinghouse reputation.

BAKED-CAKE CUSTARD has almost the same ingredients. Start the custard with the 3 cups of scalded milk poured over the 3 beaten eggs, sugar and salt, as in the preceding recipe. Add the vanilla and pour over 2 cups of coarse stale cake crumbs that have been spread in a greased baking dish. Set the dish in a pan of water and bake in a medium 350° oven for 30 or 45 minutes, until a knife blade inserted in the custard comes out clean. Cool before serving.

Plain BAKED CUSTARD is the same recipe without the cake crumbs and can be made in small greased glass or china cups, if you prefer, and 1 cup of grated cocoanut (fresh, please) added before baking, makes it naturally COCOANUT CUSTARD.

RICE COMPOTE, for four, is 2 cups of boiled rice, covered with 2 cups of stewed or canned peaches, garnished optionally with boiled custard or whipped cream. Served very cold, it is a dessert men seem to like as much, or more than their favorite RICE PUDDING but for added popularity with the opposite sex make the latter thus for four or six: Wash 3 tablespoons of rice and add to it 3 cups of milk with 4 tablespoons of sugar and ½ teaspoon of salt. Stir in ¼ teaspoon of vanilla. Bake this in a greased dish in a 325° oven for 3 hours. Stir it three or four times in the first hour or so, but this bid for male attention needs no further watching. Serve it cold with a little grated nutmeg over the surface.

CRÈME BRULÉE is a rich relative of the custard family. Scald 2 cups of thin cream in a double boiler. Beat 4 egg yolks slightly with ¼ teaspoon of salt and 1 teaspoon of sugar. Pour and stir the scalded cream over them and cook over hot water until just thick. Pour about 2 inches deep into a greased heatproof dish and let it get very cold overnight if you will. Then scatter ¾ cup of light brown sugar over the top and run the dish high up under a very hot broiler until the sugar just starts to melt. Chill thoroughly again before serving. Gourmets shuddered at this heresy—before they tested it, but fresh strawberries or sliced peaches are a wonderful addition before it goes to the table. Mrs. Rorer would undoubtedly murmur "troublesome to make" again, but then *she* never heard of this dessert.

My CHERRY RING, for four or six, calls for 1 can of big black sweet stoned cherries or 1½ cups of fresh ripe ones. If using the ripe fruit, sweeten to taste (about ¼ cup of sugar) and let simmer until their juice starts to flow. Drain the juice and add sufficient water to make 2 cups. Bring this to a boil and dissolve in it 1 package of cherry-flavored gelatine. Add the cherries. Pour into a ring mould and chill till firm. Turn from the mould and serve with 2 cups of whipped cream or vanilla ice cream in the center. Garnish the edge with cherries and top the cream with ½ cup of crushed stale macaroons.

CHERRY PUDDING for four. Take 2 cups of sour seeded canned or fresh cherries, sweetened to taste (1 cup of sugar here or even more) and simmer for 15 minutes. Drain the cherries, place in a greased baking dish and boil the juice until reduced to 1 cup. Pour over the fruit. Cream 4 tablespoons of butter with ⅓ cup of sugar, add 1 well-beaten egg, then add 1 cup of flour sifted with 2 teaspoons of baking powder and ¼ teaspoon of salt, alternately with ½ cup of milk. Pour over the cherries and juice and bake for 40 minutes in a 350° oven. Serve it hot or warm. Sour cream is good on this, as it is on all sour cherry dishes, even pie.

STRAWBERRY or PEACH SHORTCAKE, for four or six, has three versions, but starts for each with 2 cups of either fruit, crushed and sweetened, and a few additional whole berries or slices saved for a garnish. The simpler COUNTRY SHORTCAKE uses the soda biscuit dough (page 144) with 1 tablespoon of sugar added to the flour. Roll out half and put in a round cake tin. Spread with ¼ cup of melted butter and top with the other rolled half. Bake at 450° for 15 minutes. Split into halves while warm with a fork, spread the bottom half with ¼ cup of butter, put in the strawberries, cover with the other half, decorate with the reserved fruit, and serve with plenty of rich thick cream.

CITY SHORTCAKE has a layer of our old friend, sponge cake for a top and bottom and 1 cup of whipped cream over it before garnishing.

SHORTCAKE VIENNOISE with its rich foreign flavor starts with the making of a TORTE with whipped cream, a good dessert in its own right. Roll 7 unsalted large soda crackers on waxed paper until they are coarse crumbs. Beat the yolks of 4 eggs lightly with ½ cup of sugar. Add the rolled crackers, 1 cup of broken nut meats, 1 teaspoon of baking powder, and ½ teaspoon of vanilla. Fold in 4 stiffly beaten egg whites and bake in 2 greased layer cake tins for 25 minutes in a 375° oven. Put 1 cup of crushed sweetened fruit gently over one layer, then 1 cup of whipped cream, cover with the second torte and finish with the same amount of fruit and cream. Garnish with the whole fruit and hear yourself hum "The Blue Danube."

My recipe for fruitcake came to my husband down through four generations along with his determined chin, and that family feature undoubtedly helped preserve the faded paper intact through the years. Its vague instructions, including "Add 1 cup of distilled rose water but I never do" and "Taste the batter again to see if you have enough spices," made it at first a real terror and took years to standardize. Even if two or three helpers interested in sharing the proceeds make the labor go more quickly, Mrs. Rorer would always have been too ladylike to repeat my remarks on the work involved. Still I persevere, for if at least one batch of FRUITCAKE isn't baked and ripened for Christmas giving, complaints from friends and relations clutter the mail by New Year's. These quantities fill 8 bread pans but for gifts to be mailed, straight-sided pans are better, and best of all for this purpose are new glass casseroles with a lid that can be left on while the cakes are baking and help protect them afterward when journeying. Surround the wrapped cakes with heavy cardboard and wrap again in heavy brown paper before they go off to your friends. Bake in deep pans as small as 3 inches by 7 or cut the larger cakes in half after ripening, for wonderful "extras" to tuck in Christmas or birthday packages. Mine have gone half around the world in perfect condition. Gauge the weights of the dried fruit in the recipe by the statements on their packages. Don't fall for the ready sliced and packaged peels—they are *not* as good as when cut freshly. Use an electric mixer if possible for the eggs, butter and sugar, and roll up your sleeves before starting, for you'll be in to the elbows. Pick over 3 pounds of currants, 1½ pounds of seeded raisins, and 1½ pounds of the seedless variety. Cut 1 pound of seeded dates into small pieces. Shred 1 pound of candied citron and ¼ each of candied lemon and orange peel. Cut in half ½ pound of candied cherries. Mix the fruits and peels together and sprinkle over them ½ cup of rum. In another bowl, cream 1 pound of butter with 1 pound of soft light brown sugar. Beat 12 eggs until light and add to the butter and sugar, with ¾ cup of molasses and ½ cup of brandy or rye whisky, and beat again. Sift into this 4 cups of flour and 1 tablespoon each of cinnamon, nutmeg, and mace, and ½ teaspoon each of clove and allspice. Beat again. Pour the batter over the fruit and peel, and mix thoroughly until every piece is coated. Bare hands are the best implements here and a big cooking pot or dish pan the best container. Grease the chosen pans or casseroles with oil or lard. Line the bottoms and sides with heavy brown paper and grease that, too. Pat the completed cake batter gently into its pans up to the three-quarter mark. Bake the smaller cakes for 3½ hours and the large bread-pan size for 4 hours, in a 275° oven that has a pan filled with water on the bottom. Turn out of the pans and remove the paper when hot. Cool and dribble 1 tablespoon of liquor (rum sherry, whisky or brandy, but not, I beg, gin) over each cake. Stack the cakes for at least two months in a covered crock or a tin breadbox that has been lined with waxed paper, turning them over every 2 weeks or so and repeating their intoxicating dose. Whew! That was a job. It can be lightened a little at the start by baking the cakes in shifts, for the completed batter can rest in a cool place at least 24 hours, or the prepared fruit and peel can be sprinkled with liquor and left that long, too. Except the delicious cake itself, the real reward—and what a big one—of all this labor is, that made in a peaceful autumn moment a great part of your Christmas list is taken care of, inexpensively, before that harried season approaches. Decorate the cakes before using or giving away with leaves and berries of sliced citron and candied cherries, gluing them on with a syrup of ½ cup of sugar and ¼ cup of water that has been boiled until a few drops become brittle when dropped in ice water. Wrap each cake carefully in double layers of waxed paper or cellophane before tying up in holiday tissue, and, finally, hesitate before presenting one to a temperance friend, for after his finishing a large slice of my well-aged fruitcake I was once falsely accused of supplying an innocent youth with strong drink.

A piece of fruitcake steamed 1 hour makes a good pudding but real ENGLISH PLUM PUDDING is better and, like the cakes, can be made well ahead of the holiday season for home consumption or an appreciated personal gift. I actually found a three-year-old one tucked away last Christmas and it was the best we have ever had. First, line up the deep pudding bowls which may be kitchen ones of heavy china or pottery. This recipe will make 1 large, or 1 medium and 1 small pudding. The bowls should hold the batter with room to spare. For the large pudding a bowl that holds 3 quarts is about right and use bowls sized in proportion for smaller ones. Now, a little easy plain sewing. Measure the top circumference of each bowl and its top diameter and cut a piece of heavy muslin the length of the circumference and one-half the diameter, plus three inches. Seam firmly together on the diameter edge a half-inch deep and turn in and stitch the raw edges of the top and bottom. These are the bowl covers and belong in the family of good King Arthur's pudding bags. Grease the bowls. Pick over 1 pound of currants and 1 pound of raisins and cut the raisins in pieces. Shred ¼ pound of citron and ¼ pound of lemon or orange peel and dust the fruit and peel with ½ cup of flour. Beat 3 eggs with 1 cup of milk. Stir in 1 cup of flour and 2½ cups of bread crumbs (homemade ones are best) and beat again. Add the floured fruit and peel, 1½ cups of sugar, and ½ pound of ground suet. Beat well. Add ¼ teaspoon of nutmeg, ½ teaspoon each of cinnamon and salt, 1 tablespoon of grated lemon peel, and ⅛ teaspoon each of clove and mace. Then finally beat in ½ cup of brandy and ½ cup of milk. Soak the bowl covers in boiling water for a few minutes, wring them out—don't burn your fingers—and flour the inside thickly. Grease the bowls and fill three-quarters full with the batter. Now carefully pull the covers over the bottoms of the bowls until one of the hemmed edges fits just below the top. Gather and tie the muslin tightly with heavy string or tape. Stand on a rack or tin-can lid in a pot of boiling water, see that they are kept well covered with the liquid, and boil for 4 hours. These can be served direct from their original hot bath by cutting the muslin cover close to the edge of the bowl and turning out the pudding, but are much better dried and stored for a few months, and then reheated in boiling water for 1 hour. Accompany with the hard sauce (page 142) or rum- or brandy-flavored sweetened cold whipped cream. As gifts, cook them in bright-colored bowls and be sure to enclose in the package written directions for their reheating and perhaps for the hard sauce, too. Turn out the lights and surround the hot pudding with blazing sugar lumps first soaked in brandy, for a thrilling finish to a holiday meal.

PIECRUST for two covered pies. The best there is, just as good as puff paste and—hi, there, Mrs. Rorer—easy to make. Have 1 cup of lard, and ⅓ or ½ cup of butter cut in bits, both icy cold. Sift 3 cups of flour with 1 teaspoon of salt. Cut the lard into the flour with a pastry cutter or two knives until the whole is like fine meal. Add just enough ice water to hold the flour and lard together, mixing quickly with a fork, and pushing the damp sections to one side before moistening the dry. Roll lightly about ¾-inch thick on a floured board and scatter one third of the cold bits of butter over the surface. Fold in thirds, first the sides and then the ends and roll. Give the dough a quarter turn and repeat with the butter, folding and rolling. Do this once more, always rolling away from you as much as possible. Wrapped in waxed paper, this dough will keep a week in the refrigerator.

For a COVERED PIE, roll the dough about as thin as a five-cent piece, place loosely on an ungreased pie plate, and trim the edge, leaving an inch overhang, and turning this "hem" under. Brush the crust with white of egg and fill the pie with the sweetened fruit of your choice. Roll and cut a top crust 1 inch larger than the pie plate, wet the edges of the pie with cold water, adjust the top crust, turn under and press the edges firmly together with your fingers or a fork. Cut a few slashes in the top, and for fun prick in some appropriate initials too (Do you remember the story of the old lady and her "T.M." for " 'Tis Mince" or "T'aint Mince"?). Bake the pie 15 minutes at 400°, then reduce the oven heat to 350° and bake 30 minutes longer. If the filling is especially juicy, a small metal funnel inserted in the top crust before baking will keep things under control. For a BAKED PIE SHELL cover the pie plate with crust as before but leave the trimmed edge a little longer and pinch it up with your fingers into a triple-layered dam. Prick with a fork. Bake 15 or 20 minutes in a 400° oven until light brown. This is good, filled with a cooked sweetened fruit and topped with a MERINGUE made of 3 cold egg whites and a pinch of salt

beaten stiff before adding gradually 7 tablespoons of sifted powdered sugar. Flavor with ½ teaspoon of lemon juice or a few drops of vanilla. Pile on the filled pie and bake in a 300° oven for 15 or 20 minutes. Canned or fresh apple sauce, sweetened and flavored with ⅛ teaspoon of nutmeg makes a good filling under a meringue, and the same flavored and sweetened apple sauce, or the cooked fruit, alone, covered with the meringue piled in high peaks, baked and chilled and served with cream makes what I have always called BIRD'S-NEST PUDDING in spite of Mrs. Rorer and her different and difficult recipe.

For MINCE PIE use any good readymade mince meat, adding ¼ cup of brandy per pie.

Thanksgiving PUMPKIN PIE should be extra rich. Add to 1¾ cups of strained cooked pumpkin—the canned is easier—¾ of a cup of light brown sugar, 1 teaspoon of cinnamon, ½ teaspoon of ginger, ⅛ teaspoon of nutmeg, ½ teaspoon of salt, and 1 tablespoon of grated orange rind. Beat in 2 eggs and 2 cups of thin cream and 1 teaspoon of sherry. Pour this into an unbaked pie shell first brushed with egg white and bake it as directed for covered pies. Serve it warm and if it is being reheated—it keeps well for a day—dribble 1 tablespoon of melted butter over the surface before putting it in the oven. Pass the sherry, too.

Make a CUSTARD PIE with the recipe for boiled custard (page 111). Pour the raw eggs and scalded milk into the uncooked shell and bake as directed above. A cup of GRATED COCOANUT in the custard makes you know what! Meringue can be baked over any open-faced cooked pie but for our luscious pumpkin it's really too obviously lily-gilding.

Try to roll out your piecrust with as little waste as possible but any scraps can be rolled together for TURNOVERS: Cut them into 4- or 6-inch squares, put a tablespoon of jam or cooked fruit in the center of one corner, fold into a triangle, and press the dampened edges closed with a fork. Bake in a 400° oven 15 minutes. Cheese whirls (page 207) can be made with pastry scraps, too.

Pies can be prepared ahead by fitting the pie plate with its crust, wrapping carefully in waxed paper, and keeping in the refrigerator. Roll and wrap the top crust separately. When ready to cook add the filling, adjust the top, and bake as usual, for at any time, the colder the crust is before baking, the better the pie. And don't forget that pie calls for a piece of sharp cheese as a teammate.

Through the long years since Martha Washington invented it in that town, Philadelphia ice cream, like a Philadelphia lawyer, has been a smooth affair and those famous legal brains have owed a great deal to its soothing coolness.

A friend, whose family's weddings and formal parties have been served for three generations by an equally old firm of Quaker City caterers, recently dared ask its present head for the secret of their superb ice cream. "Madam," he said, serenely, "we have never had any secret. We use only the best cream."

Nevertheless, a thorough search through a large collection of modern cookbooks reveals very few recipes for ice cream that do not contain the heresy of condensed or evaporated milk, eggs, gelatin or cornstarch. And in some cooks' heaven, for there surely is one, Mrs. Rorer must be mingling her tears with those of our first President's wife as they ponder sadly on what has happened to Washington's favorite dessert. Here is why he enjoyed it and it has no equal. To make PHILADELPHIA ICE CREAM, scald 1 pint of cream (rich coffee cream is best) in a double boiler and dissolve thoroughly in it ¾ cup of sugar. Take from the stove and add 1 pint of unscalded cream. Flavor it with vanilla just to taste, from 2 teaspoons up depending on the strength of the extract, and let it get cold. Have a 2-quart freezer ready, adjust the dasher in the can, and pour in the flavored cream. Put on the top, clamp the handle firmly into place and, if you have the common female distrust of machinery, give it a few twirls just to be sure that everything is under control. Then pack the space between the can and the outside container firmly with layers of crushed ice and rock salt in the proportion of 8 to 1, turn the handle slowly and steadily for about 20 minutes until it starts to "buck" a bit, and the ice cream is frozen. Drain off any water from the ice, see that the ice itself is well below the top of the can, and remove the handle. Wipe off the top of the can carefully below its edge and remove it. Take out the dasher and if someone doesn't grab it and lick it off, scrape the ice cream from it back into the can. Then with a long wooden spoon scrape the ice cream from the sides of the can, stir and beat it well for 2 or 3 minutes, pack it down solidly, and replace the top, corking the dasher hole. Repack the freezer with ice and salt in the same proportion as before and set the freezer in a cool place, covering it with a thick layer of newspapers. Leave the ice cream for 1 or 2 hours to ripen and reach perfection. Then drain off the water again, wipe the top of the can once more, open it up, and with the first taste it will be very easy to understand why the youthful nation that originally produced it has since become a great world power.

This is one more of those basic recipes, and can be varied to individual taste or convenience, provided you remember the caterer's advice and use real cream. For CHOCOLATE ICE CREAM, break 2 squares of bitter chocolate into bits in the top of a double boiler, add 2 tablespoons of water, and melt over hot water before stirring slowly into the scalded cream and sugar. Then proceed as in the first recipe (above).

COFFEE ICE CREAM uses ½ cup of strong black coffee with the cream (above) and needs no vanilla flavoring.

FRUIT ICE CREAM, strawberry, raspberry, peach or what you will, has the fruit crushed and sweetened and allowed to stand until the juice starts to flow, before adding to unsweetened cream that has been frozen to the mushy stage. Remove the handle and top of the freezer, poke the fruit lightly around the dasher, and finish freezing and ripening as directed. The amount of fruit can vary, although for the basic 1 quart of cream, 1½ cups of fruit is a good standard.

These recipes should provide enough for six or eight people but that can't be guaranteed, as the Father of his Country certainly knew a good dish when he tasted it.

A 2-quart freezer will use about 10 pounds of ice for freezing and ripening, and if there is no local purveyor the ice can be made in the trays of an electric refrigerator. "A pint's a pound, the world around" is true here, too. The best method of crushing ice is in a heavy cloth bag with a wooden mallet or potato masher. Thick folds of newspaper or a piece of old carpet will do at a pinch to keep the cold stuff in its place, and all the work will be gladly taken off your hands by the promised reward of the scrapings from the dasher. Here's looking forward to seeing our kitchen porches once more bearing in their shade that old-time ornament, a filled freezer of real homemade ice cream.

QUICK TEA COOKIES. Cream 2 tablespoons of brown sugar with 2 tablespoons of butter. Add 1 well-beaten egg, ½ cup of sifted flour, a pinch each of salt and cinnamon, and 2 pinches of nutmeg, and beat well. Drop by small flattened spoonfuls, well apart, on a greased cooky sheet. Put a pinch of brown sugar on the top of each cookie and bake 8 minutes in a 425° oven. A teaspoon of caraway seeds can be mixed in the batter if you like the old-fashioned flavor, or a half-walnut or a sliced blanched almond placed on the top of each cooky before baking. This recipe even antedates Mrs. Rorer, coming from a very old, longhand cookbook presented to me by a farmer whose "sale" I was looking over for nonexistent antiques. The book, he said, had been his "grandmom's mom's." The cookies are soft and delicious, just spicy enough, can be mixed and baked while the kettle is coming to the boil for an unexpected guest's cup of afternoon tea, and go equally well with a glass of sherry. The recipe makes about a dozen. "Three times is *just* enough for the family" is noted underneath in surprisingly clear ink, and is still too true almost a century and a half later; as is the quaint poem that follows it:

> *Return, sweet muse, for I resign*
> *The epicurean world forever.*
> *I'd rather sup on thought divine,*
> *And please my palate never.*
> *But, changed his theme of poetry,*
> *My spouse is all for cookery.*
> *Alas, that e'en a taste for books*
> *Should change to be a taste for cooks.*

MOTHER'S SOUR-CREAM COOKIES come next in the ancient volume. Cream together ⅓ cup of butter with 1 cup of sugar. Beat in 1 egg and an optional few drops of vanilla, and ⅓ cup of thick sour cream. Add 1½ cups of flour that have been sifted with ¼ teaspoon of salt, ½ teaspoon of baking powder, and ¼ teaspoon of baking soda. Then add just enough flour to make a soft dough and chill. Not more than a half-cup extra should be necessary; remember the dough will stiffen when cold. Roll and cut out on a lightly floured board or cloth, sprinkle with sugar, bits of candied citron, raisins, or what you will, and bake at 375° for 8 or 10 minutes. These are fun to experiment with. Rolled very thin and decorated with cinnamon and sugar and slivers of almond they are SAND TARTS, a classic holiday snack. Cut into star and animal-shapes they make Christmas tree decorations that appeal to young and old much more than the usual inedible glistening baubles, although the tree itself is apt to acquire a bare look as New Year's approaches. When using the cookies thus, press an inch-long folded piece of string into an edge before baking, and watch the younger members of the family closely lest they devour the hanger with the ornament.

CRULLERS are another very old recipe and while their shape and coloring make them look like doughnuts they are much richer and taste more like cake. Cream 1 cup of butter and if you use vegetable shortening instead, add ½ teaspoon of salt. Add 1 cup of sugar, beat until thoroughly mixed. Beat in 4 eggs, one at a time, add 1 teaspoon of nutmeg, 1 cup of sour milk or buttermilk, and 1 teaspoon of soda dissolved in 1 tablespoon of water. Beat in 2½ cups of flour or just enough more to make a very soft dough. Chill thoroughly, roll out about ¾ inch thick. Cut out with a round cutter with a hole in the middle and fry in hot fat. Do not roll the unused centers back into the dough but fry them, too, for extra delicious little nubbins to snack on with a between-meal glass of milk. The fat need be no deeper than 4 inches. Turn the crullers when the undersides brown, finish frying, and drain on brown paper. Sprinkle lavishly with powdered sugar to which a tiny pinch of cinnamon may be added. These will keep at least a week in a covered crock—if well hidden.

My brother's first job took him to a small country town some miles away from home and her cherished son's constant complaints of the food served in his boardinghouse greatly upset his mother and me, too, until finally his stomach and our hearts were all eased by my sending him a carefully packed souvenir of home cooking every week or ten days. Sometimes this was a loaf of nut bread (page 145) but more often a CHOCOLATE LAYER CAKE. Melt 2½ squares of chocolate, ½ cup of butter or vegetable shortening, 3 tablespoons of strong coffee, ¼ teaspoon of salt, and 1? cups of sugar over boiling water. Let cool a little. Beat the yolk of 1 egg and 1 teaspoon of baking soda dissolved in a little water with 1 cup of sour milk or buttermilk. Beat in the chocolate mixture, mix well, and stir in gently 2 cups of sifted flour and a tablespoon of rum. Bake in greased floured pans in 1 large or 2 smaller layers at 325°; the large cake for 45 minutes, the smaller for 30 minutes. Watch carefully, for chocolate burns easily. Make a light depression with a finger in the top, and if the cake springs back it is done. Water can be used instead of coffee, and 1 teaspoon of vanilla instead of rum. A cup of chopped nuts can be added to the batter for the large cake; either way, baked in muffin tins, it makes good CHOCOLATE CUPCAKES.

Covered with whipped cream the cake is a filling dessert, but when sent to my brother I used BOILED WHITE ICING between the layers and over the top. Boil 1 cup of sugar and ¼ teaspoon of cream of tartar (or 2 teaspoons of lemon juice), and ½ cup of water until it spins a thick thread from the tines of a fork dipped in the syrup and lifted quickly out. Beat the white of an egg until stiff and slowly and carefully beat into it the hot syrup. Continue until the icing is cool and thick, flavor it with a little vanilla or almond, and spread on the cake.

CARAMEL ICING will add a homemade touch to a tasteless bakery effort and, used hot, puts such a finish on drugstore ice cream that no one will know that the entire dessert was not made in your own kitchen. It is a little rich for chocolate cake although my brother didn't think so. Boil 2 cups of brown sugar with 1 cup of top milk and a pinch of salt until it forms a soft ball in cold water. Cool, add 2 teaspoons of butter, and an optional cup of chopped nuts, and beat until of the right texture to spread. This gets a little harder after it's on the cake, so stop the beating while the icing is still soft.

Apparently my packages cheered more than one boarder, for just recently I met a most attractive man who, it turned out, had roomed next to my brother twenty-five years ago. Discovering my relationship to his former neighbor, the stranger managed to restrain himself from an embrace, but grasping my hand with fond recognition in his eyes and beaming smile, he introduced the assembled company to "the sister who made those chocolate cakes."

Beauty contestants may have their silver cups, movie picture stars their glamour and Oscars—Mrs. Rorer, Grandmother and I are content with more lasting fame.

Preserve Yourself in a Jam

Grandmother would have been shocked at the meager display—to her—of jars and bottles on my pantry shelves, but today with the groceries' canned fruits, vegetables and jellies why copy her long hot hours over a steaming preserving kettle? Homemade pickles, though, no grocery can imitate and they lend such an individual and lavish touch to the simplest meal that they are worth a few mornings in the cool autumn. Once started, try to make enough of any one kind of pickle to last two or three years. The preparation takes a little longer but the actual cooking doesn't and, as the sweet-sour stuff improves with age, this labor-saving scheme keeps a welcome variety always on hand with a minimum of effort. Use undiluted cider vinegar in cooking and economical half-pint jars for storage if your family is small. And put whole spices, when called for, in big aluminum teaballs for easy fishing out.

Just what its name says—the makings of a fine sandwich—BREAD AND BUTTER PICKLE is also good with fish, and easy to cook. Slice thinly 2 quarts of unpeeled green cucumbers and 3 medium-sized peeled onions. Separate the onions into rings and set them and the cucumbers in a bowl with ½ cup of salt and three or four fist-sized pieces of ice. Leave to crisp for 3 hours. Make a syrup of 1 quart of vinegar, 2 cups of brown sugar, 2 teaspoons of mustard seed, 1 teaspoon of celery seed and ½ teaspoon each of turmeric and cayenne pepper. Add 2 tablespoons of packaged pickling spices in a cloth bag or tea ball. Simmer for 15 minutes, add the drained cucumbers and onions, bring slowly to a full boil. Take from the fire and cool. Remove the spices and pack the pickles in sterilized jars. This will make about 4 pints.

A pinchpenny landlady refused to paint our shabby farm but I thank her just the same for two recipes for tomato pickle which have covered many a lack of flavor in cold meat or salad.

RED TOMATO PICKLE. Peel 18 large ripe tomatoes. Chop them coarsely and simmer 15 minutes. Skim off the juice for the family's breakfast. Add to the tomatoes 6 peeled onions, 2 small bunches of celery, 6 seeded green peppers, all coarsely chopped or ground, and a teaspoon each of ground cloves and allspice, ¼ teaspoon of cinnamon, 10 teaspoons of brown or white sugar, and 2½ tablespoons of salt. Let simmer until just thick, then add 1 pint of cider vinegar. Boil quickly until thick, stirring constantly, and seal in sterilized jars. This will make 10 half-pints.

Her GREEN TOMATO PICKLE, or INDIA RELISH, is equally tasty. Run the following through the coarse cutter of the food chopper: 1 peck of green tomatoes, ½ peck of peeled onions, 12 peeled green cucumbers, and 6 each of seeded green and red peppers. Mix the vegetables with 1 cup of salt and let them drain overnight, in cheesecloth or a fine colander. Next morning add 2 pounds of white or brown sugar, 1 ounce of celery seed, 2 cups of vinegar, and simmer 15 minutes, or until the vegetables are just tender. Seal in sterilized jars. This makes some 12 half-pints.

The following recipe for tomato catsup has been the pride of a Dixie Land family since "befo' de wah" and until now has never been seen by an outsider. To get it I produced a family tree, the lengthy research for which would surely have merited membership in the Colonial Dames of America. Having proved myself "kin," I was allowed to copy the directions, and now, while one half of me selfishly agrees with its original owner, the better half urges everyone to make something so delightfully different from the bought, bright red stuff. Empty beer bottles make just the right-sized containers but any small jar or bottle that can be sealed will do. Use new corks that will fit tightly and boil them and the bottles for five minutes before filling. Let the bottles cool after corking and dip the tops two or three times in melted paraffine before storing. Now for TOMATO CATSUP and having gone through so much to acquire its formula it is only a fair warning that it takes time to make. Quarter and remove any flaws from 2 pecks of ripe red tomatoes and put them in a kettle with 3 cups of chopped onion and 20 chopped cloves of garlic. Add 1 tablespoon of cayenne pepper, 3 tablespoons of whole cloves, 1 tablespoon of whole allspice, 1 tablespoon of black pepper, 2 ounces of dry mustard, ½ cup of salt and 4 cups of vinegar. Simmer for 2 hours, stirring occasionally. Remove from the fire and strain through a sieve or food mill. Return to the fire and simmer, stirring constantly, until thick, about 2 hours. An asbestos mat under the kettle is useful here to prevent scorching and the exact time of cooking is difficult to give as tomatoes vary so in their amount of juice. Just bear in mind what tomato catsup should look like, and even if yours is a little thinner or thicker the flavor will still be there. Taste for salt just before it's finished, add a little more if needed, and bottle while hot. This is a must with baked beans and codfish cakes while the younger members of the family claim that it even supplements a sandwich made with P.O.M. PICKLE (below).

GREEN GRAPE CATSUP came from a century-old home book of health, and is prescribed as a "help to the failing appetite." It is not only that, but superior to most bought meat sauces. Cover 10 cups of stemmed unripe grapes with water, simmer until soft, and press through a colander. Add 2 pints of brown sugar, 1 pint of vinegar, 2 teaspoons each of powdered allspice and cloves, 1 tablespoon of powdered cinnamon, and 1½ teaspoons each of powdered mace and salt, and ½ teaspoon of cayenne pepper. Simmer, stirring, until thick—with the asbestos pad under the kettle for added safety—and bottle and seal the same way as with the tomato catsup.

SPICED CANTELOUPE or WATERMELON RIND can be made in smaller quantities than given here and any leftover syrup saved to start the next batch. Peel and slice 1 quart of firm rind. Make a brine in the proportion of 2 tablespoons of salt to 1 quart of water. Cover the rind with this and soak it 8 hours or overnight. Drain and cover the rind with fresh water. Simmer until just tender. Make a syrup of 2 cups of cider vinegar, 1½ cups of brown sugar, 1 tablespoon each of stick cinnamon and whole cloves, and ⅛ teaspoon of allspice. Add a small piece of mace and a small piece of ginger root—the last from the drugstore. Boil for 15 minutes, then add half the prepared rind and an optional sliced lemon and simmer until the rind is clear. Put the finished rind into hot sterilized jars. Cook the rest the same way, then bring the syrup to a boil, remove the lemon if used, fill the jars with syrup, and seal.

CHUTNEY. Core, peel and slice thinly 4 cups of sour apples. Add 6 cups of sliced firm green tomatoes, 2 cups of chopped onions, 1 minced garlic clove, 1 cup of seeded raisins, and 1 tablespoon of minced candied ginger. Put in a large kettle. Add 4 cups of brown sugar, 1 cup of vinegar, 3 teaspoons of salt, 1 teaspoon of mustard seed, 1 teaspoon of ground cinnamon, ½ teaspoon of ground cloves, and ⅛ teaspoon of cayenne pepper. Simmer, stirring occasionally, until thick, about 2 hours. Seal hot in sterilized jars. This will make about 6 pints.

These pickles are good and I keep their rows well filled, but when it comes to the following mustard pickle I make astronomical quantities, for now that our family is separated, a dozen jars must sit under each Christmas tree.

Forgotten in the acclaim of *For Whom the Bell Tolls* is Ernest Hemingway's earlier *Green Hills of Africa* in which he affectionately shortens his wife's nickname of "Poor Old Mom" to "P.O.M." The year of its publication saw the same initials appear, not too mysteriously, on my automobile and other more personal articles and they have clung to this favorite relish. Its original foundation was a Pennsylvania Dutch pickle recipe given me by the trained nurse who assisted at my son's birth, and I am sure she would like to know that jars of it, wrapped in a month's Sunday comics, cheered her "baby's" lonely wartime exile in Alaska and Japan. Reader, I give you its first public appearance—the famous and sacred P.O.M. PICKLE.

Chop in bite-sized pieces 2 quarts of firm green tomatoes, 1 quart of peeled white onions, 1 bunch of celery, 2 each of seeded red and green peppers, 2 green peeled cucumbers, 1 pint of bottled sweet pickles, and 1 quart of large sour pickles. Separate the top of 1 large or 2 small cauliflowers into flowerets, chop the balance, and add both to the vegetables. Mix with ½ cup of salt, cover with water, and let stand overnight. Then just bring to a boil. Drain and return the vegetables to the kettle. Cover with a measured quantity of vinegar. For each 3 pints of vinegar allow 6 tablespoons of dry mustard, 1 tablespoon of turmeric, 3 cups of brown sugar, ½ cup of flour, and ⅛ teaspoon of cayenne pepper. Mix to a smooth thin paste with a little vinegar. Mix this with the vegetables. Put 2 tablespoons of whole allspice, 1 tablespoon each of whole cloves and cinnamon, and 2 tablespoons of mustard seed into a cloth bag or tea ball, add to the pickles, and simmer, stirring constantly, until the dressing thickens—about 15 minutes. Seal hot in sterilized jars. This is just the basic recipe. String or lima beans, boiled corn cut from the cob, and more cauliflower, can go in too, and vinegar and spices added in proportion. It will keep, covered, in a crock; and if possible let it rest 2 weeks or more before using. This is unrivaled with any meat, fish, or cheese. Chopped more finely, it is a natural for sandwiches or on crackers or toast for a quickly prepared appetizer. And let me here and now quash the rumor, started no doubt by jealous souls who do not know its secret, that in spite of the quantities we devour every year my family does *not* use it for toothpaste.

MADE MUSTARD. I found the recipe for this in an ancient volume of household hints and brought the directions up to date but the amount of vinegar is still variable. Rub together 8 tablespoons of dry mustard, 2 large minced garlic cloves and 6 teaspoons of olive oil until well blended. Add enough tarragon vinegar to make a stiff paste, then add 3 teaspoons of salt, 4 teaspoons of sugar, 2 teaspoons of pepper and ½ teaspoon of celery seed. Gradually beat in enough tarragon vinegar to make a thick batter. Give it one final beating and put into small wide-mouthed jars and cover with a thin layer of oil. Two-ounce face-cream jars are very good containers for this, odd as they sound, and the mustard will keep indefinitely. Do not fear a strong taste of garlic for that seems to vanish in the final elusive flavor.

STRAWBERRY CONSERVE is fruitier and not quite so thick as jam and has been very highly complimented by British friends. Stem 1 quart of berries— the larger the better—put in a colander and run cold water gently over them until clean. Then, just as gently, pour 1 quart of boiling water through the fruit. Drain and put in a saucepan with 1 cup of sugar and boil 5 minutes. Do not stir but shake the pan. Add 2 cups of sugar and simmer 15 minutes, still without stirring. Take from the fire and let the conserve stand overnight, then pour into sterilized jelly glasses and seal with melted paraffine.

SPICED PEACHES are a cross between preserves and pickles, are delicious with hot baked ham, and not so much trouble to make as they sound. Scald 7 pounds of slightly underripe peaches 5 minutes. Drain and plunge in cold water. Drain and remove the skins. If the peaches are really on the green side their covering may have to be helped off with a knife. Halve the peaches or leave whole, according to your fancy. Place the peaches in a deep bowl, make a syrup of 3 pounds of brown sugar, 1 pint of vinegar, and 1 ounce each of whole cinnamon and whole cloves, segregated in a cloth bag or tea ball. Bring to a boil and when the sugar is dissolved pour hot over the peaches and let stand overnight. The next day drain the syrup, boil it for 5 minutes, and pour back on the fruit. Repeat this the next two days, on the third day simmer the peaches in the syrup until just tender. Seal in sterilized jars. This makes 8 pints of halved peaches.

My Brandied Peaches are a direct hangover or result of Prohibition (remember?) when the only available intoxicant—except bathtub gin—was raw New Jersey applejack that would blow your hat in the creek when drunk straight. I still think the milder brands available now are better as a flavor in fruit than what my mother used to call "cooking brandy" and it is almost equally priced. BRANDIED PEACHES. Scald 3 pounds of firm peaches 1 or 2 minutes in boiling water and remove the skins. Halve or leave whole as you wish. Simmer a few at a time until just tender in a syrup of 1 pound of sugar and 1 cup of water. As they are finished, pack sterilized jars with the peaches, then bring the syrup to a boil, half fill each jar and then fill them up with the best apple whisky or brandy your pocketbook will stand, and seal. Pint jars will hold 4 medium-sized whole peaches and twice or three times as many halves. The amount of syrup given will make 4 to 6 pints, depending on the juiciness of the fruit. BRANDIED PEARS and CHERRIES are made the same way, using peeled and cored firm pears or stoned sweet cherries. All of these make a wonderful dessert by themselves or over vanilla ice cream.

BEACH PLUM JAM always brings memories of bright September weather and the pleading faces of earnest tousle-haired small boys offering sandy baskets of tediously picked fruit. Wash the fruit well, then just cover with water, crush lightly to start the juice flowing, and simmer until the fruit is soft. Force through a colander. Measure the pulp and add to it an equal amount of sugar. Simmer until thick, with the asbestos pad beneath, stirring constantly, then seal into sterilized jars or glasses.

WILD GRAPE JELLY brings back September, too, as well as Kipling's "Philadelphia" with "Still the grapevine scents the dusk with its soul compelling musk." Picking the fruit yourself beneath a blue fall sky is half the pleasure—that and the knowledge of the tangy accompaniment for game or meat that will follow. Therefore a big box or basket should be standard automobile equipment on any country trip after the leaves first start to turn. Wash and stem the fruit, which is best a little underripe. Put it in a kettle with water to cover the bottom, and mash until the juice starts to flow. Then continue simmering until the fruit is very soft. Strain overnight through a scalded jelly bag but do not squeeze if a clear jelly is desired. Measure the juice, return to the cleaned kettle, and boil rapidly for 10 minutes. Meanwhile heat an equal amount of sugar in the oven. Watch out, don't let it burn. Add the hot sugar gradually to the boiling juice, boil for 5 minutes longer, skim, and pour into hot sterilized glasses.

CURRANT JELLY is made just the same way and APPLE or, even better, CRAB APPLE JELLY has the washed fruit quartered, just covered with water, simmered until soft, and then strained through the bag and finished as above.

Father's favorite joke—which Mother considered a little bawdy for young ears—had to do with a puzzled flock of newly hatched chicks who discovered an orange in their nest. Finally the oldest explained "That's the orange Mama laid." My recipe for the sweet is almost as hoary and unoriginal as the story, but unlike the pun it will cheer the glummest breakfaster.

ORANGE MARMALADE. Select thin-skinned fruit. Wipe and slice into slivers 6 oranges and 2 lemons, discarding the seeds. This can be done with the coarse blade of the food chopper but a really sharp knife gives a much better appearing result. Measure the sliced fruit and add twice the quantity of water. Simmer 5 minutes, then pour into an earthen bowl and let stand, covered, overnight. The next morning, or afternoon, bring the fruit and water to a boil and simmer about 1 hour or a little longer, until the bits of rind are just tender. It can rest again for another night if more important cooking is in the offing. Then measure the fruit and its juice, add an equal amount of sugar, bring to a boil, and simmer until just thick. Old cookbooks say to tell this stage when the jam "sheets" off a spoon but constant stirring and average intelligence is really all that is necessary. Let the marmalade cool—overnight again if you wish—before spooning into sterilized glasses or jars and sealing. A grapefruit can be added to the fruit before the water and sugar, but remove the tough core and the membrane between the segments before chopping. This makes AMBER JAM. Either recipe takes a while for the cooking, so it really pays to let the work stretch through two or three days.

When our daughter was expecting her first baby, she and I whiled away the long afternoons before that much-delayed event by making the winter's supply of marmalade. The needs of two families filled a very big kettle and the simmering seemed endless but—a stern and experienced midwife—I made the poor child stand and stir. Just as we set it finally aside to cool there came the first intimation that things were happening, and I spent the early hours of the next morning in the cheerless, badly lighted waiting-room of a maternity hospital. But when I dragged home for a late breakfast, having just seen our much-desired oldest grandchild, the little girl to whom this book is dedicated, there was also the welcome sight of the finished sweet spread.

Support Your Ego with the Staff of Life

I t was bad enough when we didn't have a radio like everyone else, although it was for the simple reason that we didn't want one. It was hard to explain our family Ford touring car that we cherished for ten years, giving the faithful companion of our travels two new engines and three new tops. But if these idiosyncrasies drew raised eyebrows, the fact that I now make my own bread because, forsooth, I like to—well, that seems to have definitely put me beyond the pale. In fact, my friends have been so unanimous in their opinion about this that I sometimes get the feeling that mothers frighten their young and innocent daughters with my horrible fate unless they eat their spinach, and that total strangers look askance at me in trolleys and on the street.

And breadmaking is so much fun. I can't believe that writing deathless music or painting a really fine picture can give any greater feeling of artistic creation than gazing on a beautiful golden loaf for which you are completely responsible.

BREAD is easy, too; just as easy as 2 times 2 equals 4, and, in fact, those are the only numbers to remember all through the operation. Ready, now?

Get out a big bowl and put in it 2 crumbled yeast cakes and add 4 cups of lukewarm liquid. This can be water, cooled scalded milk, or half-and-half. Stir in 4 tablespoons of melted shortening (lard or butter), 4 tablespoons of sugar, 4 teaspoons of salt, and 4 cups of sifted flour. Beat this batter hard for 2 minutes. Stir in 4 more cups of sifted flour and then see how little more flour you can add and still have a workable dough. Two cups may do it, and you shouldn't need more than 4. Dust a breadboard or cloth with flour—always sifted, please. Dump the dough on the board and dust with ½ cup of flour.

Now relax. Sit down, light a cigarette, write a letter or make your own plans for the next 15 minutes while the dough "tightens up" as we bakers say. I generally improve this shining quarter-hour by washing the mixing bowl, and like the fisherman's suspenders in Kipling's "How the Whale Got His Throat," which you are implored to remember, you'll see why later, "oh, best beloved."

Is your cigarette finished? Let's go. This is fun. Start to knead by punching the dough away from you, then pull it toward you and press down. Give it a quarter-turn and repeat the preceding act for 10 minutes or a little longer. Add just enough flour to keep the dough from sticking to your hands or the board, and before you know it, you'll have a satin-smooth elastic mass which, believe it or not, is your bread. Put into your clean mixing bowl—you see now why you washed it—4 tablespoons (remember the magic number 4) of shortening or oil. Place the dough in the bowl and turn it till every part of the surface is covered with the grease. Then cover the bowl with a damp towel or napkin and leave it in a warm spot for 4 hours. It should double its size or a little more.

For a whole morning or afternoon go your ways, for what you have hidden is practically foolproof. If you wish, take a peek in about 2 hours just to see if things are progressing, but don't be disappointed if they seem slow. Like the watched pot boiling, dough seems to get active just when you've given up hope. Now for more fun. When your dough has doubled in size, attack it right in its bowl. Pretend it's your worst enemy and give it a great punch right in the solar plexus to deflate its ego. Give it a couple more good lefts and rights and remove it from the bowl to the floured breadboard and cut it into quarters. There, madam, are four loaves of bread. Let them stand a few minutes for another tightening. Shape them up and they are ready for the pans. Grease 4 pans 5 by 10 inches (glass or metal) and then place a loaf in each pan. Grease the top of each loaf and then put the pans back in the same warm spot for at least 2 hours during which time they will more than double their original size. Again, don't worry about them falling for they won't, honestly. And they are better too high than too low. Have your oven ready at a good 375° and put in the bread. Bake it 15 minutes and then turn the heat down to 350°. Bake the loaves for ½ hour longer, and here again too much is better than too little. When done, loaves don't need any help to get them out of their pans. Now get really excited. Take out your loaves, turn them out on a cake rack or clean towel, then—sniff, throw out your chest, and pat yourself on the back. And if you can resist cutting off a big warm piece and spreading it thickly with butter you're not the girl I think. If you like a crusty loaf, leave the bread to cool uncovered. For a soft outside, tuck a clean towel over the loaves until cool.

Four lovely loaves of bread are lesson number one. But don't stop there, for you are just beginning. Try making only two loaves and using the other half of the dough for rolls.

DINNER ROLLS. Put 4 tablespoons of melted butter or cooking oil in a soup plate or saucer. Pinch off bits of dough. Form into small balls about the size of an English walnut. Dip each into the grease. Then march them in a double row, not too closely spaced, down a greased bread pan. (A cake pan will do but I like the narrow shape better because it gives an outside crust on every roll.) Let rise 1 hour and then bake a little less time than loaves, about 20 minutes. If you plan to reheat the rolls before serving, take them from the oven when pale gold and let them get their tan again in the oven just before they come on the table, warm and crusty, nested in a folded napkin.

POCKETBOOK ROLLS. Roll dough ¼ inch thin; cut in 2-inch circles; dip in (or brush with) melted butter or cooking fat and fold in half with the upper edge not quite over the lower. Place them in a greased pan, not touching, and finish as dinner rolls (above).

SALT STICKS. Roll and cut the dough into thin 2-inch triangles; grease them; roll them up with the broad side inside and sprinkle with coarse salt and caraway seeds. Finish as dinner rolls (above).

CLOVERLEAF ROLLS are each three small balls of dough the size of marbles, rubbed between buttery palms and put in greased muffin tins. Finish as dinner rolls (above).

Now that you've passed your apprenticeship with flying colors and had lots of fun, we're going on to even further, but just as simple, fields. Again take just one half the dough for your two loaves or rolls. Take the other half, put it back into the bowl, and with your hands mix in 1 whole egg, 4 tablespoons sugar, and 4 tablespoons melted butter. Then add 1 cup sifted flour. Perhaps less flour will do, or perhaps a little more will be needed. It must bring your dough back to the soft but firm state of the dough in your loaves. With this, you start on a new "Cook's Tour" of discovery, for what you have here is SWEET DOUGH and, oh, the wonderful things you can make with it!

Let's start with CINNAMON BUNS—and these will be the real old-time Philadelphia "Stickies"—the ones you make for homesick out-of-town relatives.

First, the sticky part. Put in an iron skillet 2 cups granulated sugar and add 4 tablespoons butter. Stir constantly over a medium fire until you have a thick light golden syrup, and watch it carefully for it burns easily. Add slowly 1½ cups hot water and replace over the heat. Keep stirring till the sugar is dissolved. It should look like a pale maple syrup. Pour this into two greased bread pans, dividing it evenly, and start on the buns themselves. Roll ½ of the sweet dough into an oblong about ¼-inch thick, 7 or 8 inches wide, and 14 to 20 inches long, and spread this with 1 cup (or a little over) of brown sugar and ½ teaspoon cinnamon. Scatter it with 1 cup of seedless raisins or currants or a mixture of both and a few slivers of preserved citron, too, if you like. Then dot the whole liberally with butter. Roll it up like a jelly roll, pressing the far edge into the last fold. Cut the roll into 2-inch pieces and set each piece carefully, a cut side up, in the syrup, about six or eight to a pan, but give them plenty of room. Repeat on your second half of dough. Let the buns rise 2 hours or until light and bake in a 375° oven for 20 or 25 minutes until the buns are brown on top and the rich syrup has oozed delightfully up over their sides. Turn them upside down on a dish as soon as

they are done, and spoon any extra syrup over the top. Let them cool as long as you can keep from sampling one, with a glass of milk or cup of coffee (or until the family sniffs the delicious odor and descends upon them).

Make COFFEE CAKE the same way, using a little less brown sugar and no cinnamon. Form one roll into a circle, pinch the ends firmly together, and make 4 or 5 slashes halfway through the top. Put the roll on a cooky sheet. Let it rise, and then put into the same 375° oven for the same length of time. Ice this while it is hot with very little confectioner's sugar mixed to a thin paste with hot water or milk.

COFFEE CAKE NUMBER 2 is made from a cup of sweet dough rolled to fit a bread pan and topped with ¼ cup brown sugar, ¼ cup flour mixed with 2 tablespoons melted butter, ½ cup of chopped nuts, and a speck of cinnamon.

COFFEE CAKE NUMBER 3 is made from half the recipe for sweet dough with ½ cup of cut-up candied cherries, ¼ cup of raisins, and 1 tablespoon of citron kneaded into it. Roll it into a flat round about 2 inches thick. Fold it like an omelet and let it rise on a flat baking pan before baking.

CHRISTMAS LOAF has the same fruits as above. Form the sweet dough into a big loaf, and you have the delicious bread that all Italian stores sell at holiday time.

HOLIDAY CAKES. Roll out a thin piece of sweet dough and try your hand at art in the way of animals and figures for the children and grown-ups, too. We always have what passes for an angel at each place, Christmas morning. The recommended way is to make a paper pattern and cut around it, but freehand drawing with a small sharp knife is just as effective and adds that homey amateur touch. Make the eyes of currants or raisins, mouths (and even ears) of citron or slices of red cherries. Santa Claus has a white beard and hair of confectioner's sugar and milk icing, with cherry buttons down his famous round belly. Bread rabbits come with Easter, or ducks, or a rooster with a cherry-studded comb, and I once even produced a reasonable facsimile of a bicycle for a small boy who was waiting hopefully to see what was under the tree.

APPLE DESSERT—it has no other name in our family—can be tossed into the oven in a twinkling, right under the eye of the unexpected guest, who marvels at your skill. Roll a piece of sweet dough as thin as you can and put it in a square greased biscuit pan. Then set peeled and cored eighths of tart apples close together over the surface. Top with brown sugar—the amount depending upon the sweetness of the apples—a shake of nutmeg and a few dots of butter. Let it rise in a warm place for 45 minutes while you get dinner. Bake it in an oven at 375° for about 25 minutes. Serve it warm and fresh from the oven, and with it cream, or vanilla ice cream, or the HARD SAUCE which my grandmother used to make. Into ½ cup of soft butter she beat as much confectioner's sugar as it would hold. She flavored it with vanilla for us children, or rum for the grown-ups. Have it ice cold to contrast with the hot Apple Dessert.

After the first rising and kneading you can either make up your loaves and any sweet dough breads or desserts, or you can put your dough in the icebox, where it will keep fresh for 3 or 4 days, to use a little at a time or all at once as you wish. Be sure to remember always to see that the whole surface of the dough and the bowl too is well greased. Always keep a cover on the bowl or crock and punch the dough down every 8 hours or so. When you are ready to use it give it one final whack and proceed as though the dough were freshly made, allowing a little extra time for it to rise after its chilly rest before it goes in the oven.

The same recipe for dough made in the evening with only 1 yeast cake will take overnight to rise. The mixing uses time after dinner, of course, but it's a fine welcome sight early in the morning of baking day. If you don't want to set to work on it before breakfast, keep it in its place by a well-directed smack, cover, and wait to start kneading until your dishes are out of the way.

Any dough will rise more quickly if set in a pan of warm (not hot) water halfway up the sides of its container. Cover and watch it carefully for this is likely to hurry things surprisingly.

POTATO BREAD is made with lukewarm water in which potatoes have been boiled, and a small hot mashed potato, about ½ cup, added before the flour and other ingredients. Many cooks think that this makes a lighter loaf and it is supposed to keep fresh and moist longer. It's worth giving a try, now that you are so skillful.

If you have used up all your bread dough in loaves, and I wouldn't blame you, here is a recipe that will make somewhat richer rolls than your originals and is good for cinnamon buns and coffee cake, too. It was given to me as ICEBOX SWEET DOUGH, though it is no more at home in the icebox than the others. Pour 1 cup of boiling water over ¾ cup of lard and butter mixed, add 1 teaspoon of salt and 4 tablespoons sugar. Then add 1 cup of cold water. If the mixture seems hot let it stand till lukewarm. Add 1 yeast cake, crumbled into ¼ cup of lukewarm water, 3 cups of sifted flour, and 2 eggs. Beat well, then beat in 3 or 4 cups more flour to make a very soft dough. Knead it for just a few minutes on a floured board, coat it thoroughly with grease, and let rise, covered, for 2 hours. Punch it down and form it into what you will, letting it rise again 2 hours before baking. This dough keeps beautifully in its greased covered bowl, but demands a longer rising period after being chilled.

For PLAIN DOUGHNUTS take ½ the recipe for either sweet dough (page 140), knead in ½ teaspoonful of nutmeg, roll out ½ inch thick, and cut with a floured cutter. Let them rise 1 hour on a lightly floured board or towel. Fry in deep hot fat, a few at a time, drain on brown paper, and dust with powdered sugar.

Below Mason and Dixon's line the mealtime slogan is, "Take two and butter them while they're hot." SODA BISCUITS are one of the hot breads responsible for this maxim: Blend 2 cups of flour sifted with 4 teaspoons of baking powder and 1 teaspoon salt, with 2 tablespoons of lard, butter, or half and half, until it looks like coarse meal. Use a pastry mixer, two knives, or your fingers. Add 1 cup milk, or a little less, for a soft dough. Roll out on a floured board and shape with a floured cutter. Bake in a 450° oven about 10 minutes. For DROP BISCUITS add enough more milk to make a thick batter, drop or push off the tip of a spoon onto a greased cooky sheet, and bake at 450° for 10 minutes. For your own biscuit mix, keep the blended flour, baking powder, salt and shortening in a covered jar in the icebox and add the milk just before baking.

SPOON BREAD is another Southern specialty and I am not sure that the Confederate insistence that only water-ground white cornmeal be used in its preparation didn't help precipitate the War Between the States for most "damn Yankees" prefer the yellow. Don't let's argue but begin by pouring 2 cups of boiling water over 1½ cups of the meal of your choice. Stir and let cool. Add 2 tablespoons melted butter, 2 egg yolks, 1½ cups sour milk or buttermilk mixed with 1 teaspoon of soda and 1 of salt. Beat well, then fold in the stiffly beaten egg whites. Bake this in a deep greased dish for

45 minutes at 400°. A few strips of bacon on top before baking add flavor. Here's a traditional Dixie Land side partner of fish.

SOUR MILK MUFFINS. Beat 1 egg yolk, add 1 cup sour milk. Stir in 1 cup flour sifted with ½ teaspoon baking soda, 1 teaspoon sugar and 1 teaspoon salt. Fold in the beaten egg white and 1 tablespoon oil or melted butter. Pour into small greased muffin tins and bake at 400° for 10 minutes.

My recipe for nut bread came from a friend's older sister. She had been to college, not such a usual occurence twenty-five years ago, and filled our jealous young ears with tales of gay "cocoa and kimono" parties after "lights." The modest kimono has been superseded by pajamas and her directions for cocoa which included lots of sweetened condensed milk and a topping of marshmallows (!) sound much too rich for our present diet-conscious collegians, but the NUT BREAD is just as simple to make and as good to eat as ever. Beat 1 egg into ½ cup sugar. Add a cup of milk and stir in 2 cups flour sifted with 1 teaspoon salt and 2 teaspoons baking powder; beat, then stir in 1 cup of broken nut meats (2 cups if you want it extra nutty). Put in a greased bread pan, let it rest 30 minutes, and bake in a 350° oven for 45 minutes.

This cuts better if it is made a day ahead, which is easier to say than do. I well remember leaving a supposedly invalid husband and two freshly made loaves of nut bread on separate floors, only to discover on my return that one loaf and almost a quarter of the second had been used as a recuperative afternoon snack. Arguments that nut bread was not included in the prescribed "light diet" were answered by a well-fed smirk and my sympathy vanished as rapidly as my loaves. Strangely enough a quick cure was effected and the patient—though why that word should be applied to the average ailing male!—was up and about and on his way to his office the next morning. A story with a moral which you will appreciate after your own first baking. Any bread is easy to make but hard to keep.

"Open Your Mouth and Say 'Ah-ha'"

O ur daughter insists that her range has a folding top over its burners for the sole purpose of turning the entire thing into an invalid's bed table, and many another harried young mother will wholeheartedly agree that a mortal illness is her only chance of seeing an idle stove.

Ridiculous as it seems, our child's basic idea is sound, for while the stove itself might be an awkward addition to a sickroom, the food it furnishes is always so welcome to the bedridden that no cook need ever give way to the desperate "What shall I send?" feeling that so often comes after visiting a friend who is, as the old books say, languishing on a bed of pain. There he or she reclines, surrounded by what seems to be the entire contents of a florist's window, and the thought of the small bouquet that you plan to add to the collection dies aborning. Don't despair. You can show your sympathy in an original way which will be much more appreciated. Go home and take a look into your preserve closet. There! See those lovely jars of brandied peaches (page 133) you worked away at last summer. Wrap one in your fanciest gift paper, stick a few garden flowers or a spicy carnation in the perky ribbon bow, and you won't have long to wait for almost pitifully enthusiastic thanks.

No peaches left? A glass or two of your own strawberry jam (page 132) will be just as welcome and might be accompanied by tiny jars of homemade pickle (page 127) to add a tang to dull hospital fare.

What? No preserves at all? Fie, remember to make more next year and turn your attention to comforting the invalid with some real WINE JELLY. Soak 1 envelope of Gelatine in ¼ cup of cold water. Squeeze the juice of 1 lemon, sweeten it slightly, and be sure the sugar is thoroughly dissolved. Put the gelatine into ¾ cup of boiling hot water and stir until not a trace of the granules is left. Add the sweetened lemon juice and 1 cup of the driest and best sherry or port wine you can afford. Taste the jelly for sugar, strain, pour into your prettiest bowl or a jar, and chill. Then wrap, tie and decorate the package as directed above before delivering it to the grateful recipient, whom it will delight more than all the orchids ever flown from the tropics.

Next, send the sick one a bowl of fresh fruit compote, made as on page 176. Leave out the liquor and attach to the package instead a miniature bottle of peach or apricot brandy, ready to add its little exotic touch and flavor to the fruit if the patient is permitted the dissipation.

And how about a small delicate sponge cake (page 110) with a "Get Well" wish iced on its surface?

Homemade soups always appeal to an invalid—*vide* the onion soup on page 43—as does a small jar of cold pressed chicken (page 51) or perhaps the minced white meat covered with Newburg sauce (page 96) with a tiny bottle of sherry beside it. Other ideas are a bottle of French dressing (page 100) and a big ripe avocado pear to go along, or a plate of iced oysters on the half-shell and a bottle of tomato catsup, (page 129) delivered, with your card, just before lunch or dinner.

My infrequent youthful illnesses were always cheered by the knowledge that as soon as the doctor pronounced his dread verdict of "bed," cups of delicious steaming BEEF TEA would appear to start bolstering my supposedly waning strength. Modern medical men no longer consider this nourishing, but it's mighty tasty, appetite-teasing, and easily digested. Remove all the fat from 1 pound of top or bottom of the round and sear on one side on a hot, very, very lightly greased skillet, or under the broiler. Cut into ½ inch cubes and place in a double boiler. Cover with 2 cups of cold water and let rest for 2 hours. Cook, tightly covered, over just simmering water for 2 hours more. Strain and press the meat in a potato ricer to extract every drop of juice. Salt slightly and serve it hot—but not boiled—or icy cold. The convalescent will relish a few delicate pieces of Melba toast on the side.

Too few people remember that a sick person is really a hostess in her small room, so as soon as the "No Visitors" sign is down send the invalid something both she and her guests can enjoy. This is the moment to bring forth a well-aged fruitcake or a pan of cinnamon buns or tiny homemade crullers. With the sitting-up-and-taking-notice stage well along, gladden the invalid's heart with a box of cheese whirls (page 207) and a bottle of Champagne when the doctor allows it. A bottle of fine whisky or sherry is an equally good lifter-upper, especially if an old-fashioned topless thimble (from the notion counter) comes with it, and a fake prescription to "Drink a thimbleful three times a day until improvement." Men love this gift.

When the patient has returned home and is "up and about but not out" comes the time to share with her your birthday cake, or that extra delicious dessert, or the main dish that has turned out particularly well. Or find out whether a restricted diet has been ordered and offer to provide an entire meal—either lunch or dinner. Send or bring it set out in your daintiest china on your prettiest tray. Both the invalid and the nurse will consider themselves in your debt, one for the lightening of her labor, the other for the bringing of that variety which is the spice of life, sick or well.

If you do send flowers, see if you can't arrange to have your offering already in the room when the patient arrives at the hospital. I know that the small bouquet I found waiting on the otherwise bare bureau did more to allay my quivering nerves than any of the more elaborate offerings I got later.

Perhaps the height of originality in invalid gifts was the large mourning wreath presented to my father-in-law just as he was well out of the woods after a most serious operation. A pretended forgotten order, it had "No Cross, No Harp" in large gilt letters on its hideous lavender bow and it decorated (though perhaps that is not quite the word) a foot-post of his high white bed until he recovered. I've always felt the giver and receiver both had a rather warped sense of humor but the funeral gift was certainly enjoyed.

Instead of such a grisly object, bring your convalescent a few copies of the newest slick-paper magazines, fashion news for a woman and *Esquire* or *Fortune* for a man. Both sexes will relish a package of twenty-five cent detective stories, and any unfortunate in for a long siege will get unlimited amusement from one of the old-fashioned almanacs that many newsstands still sell. You might send this with a note offering to take either end of a small wager as to whether the weather prognostications are correct during the time your friend is on the shelf, and then put in a call once in a while to see how your share of the "pool" is progressing. A real "outside" interest.

Young bloods will take to a big package of their favorite comic books, horrible as they seem to grown-ups, and a pile of movie magazines is sure to delight an ill high school girl, no matter how serious minded she is when in full health. Her dressy sister will get hours of pleasure out of a box of artificial fingernails from the five-and-ten, accompanied by trial sizes of nail polish in the newest shades. Tuck in three or four small different-colored lipsticks, too, for a really glamorous gift to a young lady.

The very small sick-a-bed will be enraptured by a goldfish in its bowl, or the glass bubble may hold one of those remarkable baby turtles that pet shops sell all ready to be decorated with the recipient's name; but don't, as I once did, send the latter to a child in isolation with a contagious disease, for long, loud wails rent the air when, with the patient fully recovered, the beloved companion of the illness had to be destroyed. Little youngsters, bless them, love lots of little presents and a dollar's worth from Woolworth's, wrapped separately and arranged in a box like a Jack Horner Pie, gives the young invalid much to look forward to. Tag each string or ribbon with the hour or day in which it is to be pulled (perhaps after medicine) and the mother's or nurse's blessings will rain on your head. If the doctor allows, a package of candy sticks or lollipops answers the same purpose.

After all, the very best present you can give a sick friend is a bit of yourself. Two short cheery visits are better than one long wearying call and even the most lonely sufferer will feel cheered and popular if you flatter her by phoning or writing ahead to make an "appointment." If you do this, keep your date come hell or high water, for invalids, like small children, take disappointment bitterly to heart and the nonappearance of an expected friend has caused many a setback on the road to recovery. Evening, after the usual dreadfully early hospital supper, is a good time to drop in, for it helps the homesick feeling that comes oftenest before settling down for the night. Hospitals, or sickrooms generally, aren't happy places at best and a few laughs and perhaps a hand of gin rummy with an old friend will do more than pills to bring an easy rest and a bright outlook for next morning.

ADDITIONAL SUGGESTIONS FOR INVALID GIFTS

Eatables should be in individual portions (unless you're certain of the invalid's appetite) and always attractively wrapped and garnished.

- THIN SLICES OF VIRGINIA HAM (page 157). Top the package with a tiny china pig and a message like "Greetings from one to another."
- A SMALL LOAF OF BREAD or NUT BREAD or a PAN OF BISCUITS (pages 137, 145, 144).
- TOMATO JELLY (page 161).

- Two lightly seasoned STUFFED EGGS (page 154) wrapped in frilly waxed paper.
- CUSTARD PIE or a BAKED CUSTARD (page 119, 111). This might come from "Charlie Chaplin."
- TRIFLE (page 111).
- CLAM BISQUE (page 42).
- A split of CHAMPAGNE and a tiny jar of CAVIAR. Wonderful for the last night in hospital.
- A jar of CURRIED CHICKEN (page 173) and lots of little packages of side dishes (make the sauce mild).
- A miniature bottle of WHISKY made into an old-fashioned bouquet with a border of fresh mint and the frill of a paper doily. Substitute a jar of LEMONADE (page 204) for the alcoholic beverage if necessary.
- VEAL AND HAM PIE (page 57) with a Union Jack stuck in the top.
- And for old or young, always ICE CREAM (page 120).
- These last few suggestions are for the rare moments when you are uncertain of the invalid's tastes or appetite.
- A book on SOLITAIRE and a DECK OF CARDS.
- A prickly CACTUS plant, with a card attached "I'm coming to sit on this until you get well."
- A bottle of EAU DE COLOGNE or a box of LAVENDER or PINE-SCENTED SOAP.

Egg Yourself on in Emergencies

Our favorite overnight tourist camp in New England has a sign in the dining room that bears the mystic message "Eggs Anyways," but it was Mary MacHugh, bless her Scotch heart, who really taught me that first principle of the emergency shelf. By then the two children were grown up, I had acquired a job, and Mary took us and what my conservative brother-in-law called our "country club"—with reason, I am afraid—under her wing for two blissful years. Then "Me laigs is givin' out, mum,"—small wonder, too, and "as good cooks go, she went."

Wherever Mary is now, my thankful prayers followed her, when during the war, my husband was a ship-building inspector for the Navy. He left early each morning for a shipyard and we had no phone. At least once a week a station wagon in all its glory of battleship-gray paint drove down our farm lane well before our regular lunchtime and disgorged at the door not only the expected man of the house but two or three nice—and hungry—young ensigns, and frequently the captain who was chief officer of the naval district, a charming man and the acknowledged gourmet of Annapolis.

Then it was that my thoughts went back to Mary and the peaceful day long before when arriving home once after lunch, I saw from the wreckage on the dining-room table that not only my college son but others had partaken of what, I supposed, had been a sparse menu.

"Eight boys there was, mum, and all hungry from that rowin'. Don't you worry. I just give the lot of 'em aigs. Aigs is always handy in a house where there's boys." And that last sentence, with "boys" supplanted by "unexpected guests," should be emblazoned on every refrigerator, painted on every kitchen wall, and learned by heart by every potential hostess.

Hard-boiled eggs are perhaps the best helpers-out, and if you have frequent unexpected guests it isn't a bad idea to keep a half-dozen or so ready in the icebox. They can be stretchers for almost any creamed dish, such as chicken, dried beef, or plain hash, and can hardly be bettered by themselves, sliced in a curry (page 173) or in a well-seasoned white sauce (page 94), topped with the green of chopped chives or parsley. The family salad looks a little gayer, and goes further, with two or three put through the potato ricer and sprinkled on top.

STUFFED EGGS will make any dish of cold meat or salad appear more lavish. Cut hard-cooked eggs in half, mash the yolks well, and season highly with a bit of scraped onion, dry mustard, a small dash of Worcestershire sauce and plenty of tart vinegar with salt and black pepper. Heap this mixture into the empty whites, dust the tops with a bit of paprika, and there you are.

EGGS CHIMAY, delicious but no emergency dish, belong here only as a guide. Plain stuffed eggs (above) make a very fine hurried foundation, and the mushrooms can be replaced by deviled ham or caviar. Wash, but do not peel, ¼ pound mushrooms and grind or chop them finely. Sauté them 5 minutes over a medium heat in 2 tablespoons butter with 1 tablespoon each of chopped chives and parsley. Add salt and pepper to taste. Halve 6 hard-boiled eggs lengthwise and mash the yolks well. Add the mushroom mixture, taste for seasoning, and heap it in the halved whites. Place yolk side up on a greased shallow baking dish. Cover with white sauce (page 94) and dust with 2 tablespoons grated Parmesan cheese, 2 teaspoons bread crumbs, and a few bits of butter. Bake in a 400° oven for 15 minutes.

An OMELET is one of the more perfect luncheon dishes whether you are facing an emergency or not. My grandmother always maintained "Only a lady could make one," but while I know I've come far from her definition of gentility, her old recipe of 2 eggs, ½ egg shell of milk or cream, a shake of salt, pepper, and flour, per person, still works. Beat the yolks slightly, add milk, flour and seasonings, then add the slightly beaten whites, and mix well.

Have an iron skillet hot and the bottom covered with a good layer of melted butter, and turn the pan so that it runs well up on the sides. Put in the omelet and as soon as it starts to set move to a low heat. Keep lifting the cooked part gently with a knife to let the raw egg run under, and just before it's done put it in a medium oven for a few minutes. The top should be just solid. Rolling the finished product is a knack that unfortunately comes easily only with practice, but try grasping the pan in your left hand, standing it almost upright on the hot serving dish, and giving the top part of the omelet a start with a spatula or cake turner. The result should be almost professional.

The famous French OMELETTE AU FINES HERBES is just the same recipe, with a tablespoon or so of finely minced chives or green onion tops and parsley, and perhaps a few leaves of tarragon and a tiny pinch of thyme, mixed in the eggs, and I hope I don't have to tell you that a SPANISH OMELET has stewed tomatoes—leftover or fresh—mixed with chopped onions and some sliced stuffed green olives oozing from its folds. Chopped green peppers can go in this, too. A can of green asparagus tips, or string beans, are good heated and rolled in either the plain or fines herbes model, and try a small cupful of leftover chicken, ham, or both, put through the coarse grinder or just chopped finely and mixed with plenty of white sauce (page 94), as a filling. For a very de luxe version, fold in red or black caviar, top the finished product with sour cream, and herald OMELET ROMANOFF.

And JELLY OMELET for a quick dessert! Make a plain omelet (above) but go easy on the salt and no pepper. Break up a glassful of tart currant or grape jelly with a fork, use it as a filling, dust the top plentifully with granulated sugar, and slide the whole dish for a minute into a hot oven to start the jelly melting. If you wish, pour a few teaspoons of rum or brandy over the top and bring it to the table flaming. Peach or apricot jam is good in this, too.

If you like FLUFFY OMELETS, and a few eggs do go a long distance cooked that way, allow only 1, or perhaps 1½ eggs per person. Beat the whites, with a pinch of salt, till dry and ready to stand in peaks, then pour your beaten yolks over them, and fold over and over carefully. Then into a buttered skillet, and after the bottom just sets, put it into a hot oven for about fifteen minutes. The best trimming for this is brown, crisp bacon, and it must be served at once. As a matter of fact no omelet likes to be kept waiting too long.

CHEESE SOUFFLÉ. Melt 1½ cups of grated sharp cheese in 2 cups of white sauce. Add ½ teaspoon of salt and a few grains of cayenne. Let cool and beat into 4 egg yolks. This part may be made ahead. When ready to cook fold in 4 stiffly beaten egg whites and pour into a greased baking dish. Set in a shallow pan of water and bake at 350° or 325° for 1 hour. 2 tablespoons of cooked chopped bacon are good in this.

POACHED EGGS are not only invalid food, as so many people seem to think, but a fine luncheon dish, too. Have the water for them boiling and deep enough to cover, with an inch or so to spare. Add a tablespoon of vinegar and the same of salt to each quart, slide the shelled eggs carefully in, cover, and keep the heat very low for 5 minutes. Dropping a few "poaches" on the kitchen floor, with vain cursing of the usual flat egg turner, led to the discovery that the best instrument for removing them from their hot bath is a large slotted mixing spoon. Have all your trimmings for the eggs ready before you start poaching. Serve the eggs on toast with one of the ready-canned tomato sauces and a few pieces of bacon or frizzled ham. Leftover spinach can be used under them, too, and a white sauce (page 94) laced with plenty of snappy cheese is good on top, or you can just let the cheese melt in the oven on the toast and put the egg and tomato sauce on top of that. For a more elaborate dish, try a thick slice of broiled tomato on a toasted half of an English muffin, top it with a poached egg and the cheese sauce with bacon again as a garnish.

I hope I don't have to remind you of the old reliable EGGS BENEDICT— a toasted English muffin plus a slice of Virginia ham topped with a poached egg and hollandaise sauce (page 97) over all. I was first introduced to this at Philadelphia's famous old L'Aiglon Restaurant and while I long ago mastered its uncomplicated recipe it still remains, in my opinion, a most glamorous dish.

Talking of VIRGINIA HAM—there is the perfect emergency ration. Really expensive to start with, I grant you, but such an article as to lean your back against. My last one cost $6, fed eight people at a buffet supper, and remained a comfort in the icebox for snacks, salads, sandwiches and "ekeings" for almost three months longer. Get one between 10 and 15 pounds. The larger ones are likely to have too much fat and be too difficult to handle, although they can be cut in half, while a smaller weight generally has too much bone to be really economical. To prepare one, take it out of its cotton bag and paper wrapping, if it comes that way, and with your stiffest vegetable brush scrub the whole thing thoroughly in a dishpan or sink full of water. If it seems particularly old and mouldy—a good sign—repeat the process with fresh water. Now fill up whatever pot you are going to boil it in and if you have no regular ham boiler don't despair—an old wash boiler, or a canner, or a big pressure cooker will do. Soak your treasure at least 12 hours, or, if you have an antique, 24 hours with a change of water once is better. I've never been able to see any difference in whether the skin of the ham was up or down, although experts say "up." After soaking, refill the big cooking pot, and if you're using a pressure cooker leave the lid ajar, put in the ham, see that it's well covered with water, and bring it to a low boil over a slow fire. Let it just simmer about 30 minutes to the pound and keep the water well up. When it's done, a fork goes in easily and the end bone feels a little loose. Let it cool in the water it was cooked in, and then lift it tenderly out and carefully peel off the skin. Put it fat side up in a baking pan and score the fat into inch squares. Mix 1 cup brown sugar with 2 tablespoons of English mustard, and cover the ham with it. Get it well into the scored cuts. Now insert a whole clove into each square and slide the ham into a 350° oven for about 30 minutes, basting it from time to time gently with a little of the water in which it was boiled, or cider or sherry. When it's brown and glazed let it get cool before its trip to the icebox for a thorough chill. Then approach it respectfully with your sharpest carver and watch the delicate pink slivers fall from the knife.

Any country-smoked ham appreciates the same treatment, and don't forget that the place to keep your uncooked smoked ham is in the cellar, not the refrigerator.

The second inexpensive assistant to have in your icebox for quick meals is cold boiled potatoes, dull as it sounds, but their variations are almost as endless as those of eggs. Hashed Browns are my first thought, probably because I spent most of my young summer days on the New Jersey coast and a plate of crusty potatoes, soft inside and turned omelet-fashion from the sizzling pan always brings back memories of numerous fishing picnics and I can almost smell the driftwood smoke and see the sun setting over the water. The party generally consisted of three or four young sportsmen and the fortunate (so we thought) girls of their choice, and we started early and eagerly planning and providing food for our Izaak Waltons. First, we'd have two stuffed eggs apiece, made as I have told you, each half carefully clapped onto its mate and the whole wrapped in wax paper. Then a quart jar or so of whole peeled ripe tomatoes and a smaller one of sharp French dressing, thick with slices of onion and chopped celery, and perhaps a washed, chilly head of lettuce, well wrapped. One of the embryo housewives would produce a cake or a pie, for in those days girls thought their swains were impressed by their culinary skill, and with a great paper bag of cold boiled white potatoes and a pound or two of sliced bacon we were ready to go, accompanied by rattling frying pans, plates, cups, cutlery and a coffee pot. A trip by canoe or sailboat to the beach, and the boys busied themselves building a fire and then vanished with their fishing rods while we got ready for their return in what we felt was a truly domestic fashion. Coffee and water were measured into the big pot and set aside. The tomatoes and dressing were put in a shady, cool place, bread was sliced and buttered, and all hands began peeling and dicing the potatoes. At dusk, just before we expected our fishermen back, we started all the bacon frying and then put the brown slices to drain on a bit of paper. Some of the grease was saved for the fish that seemingly never failed to appear with the boys and into about ½ inch of the grease that was

left went the diced potatoes and a few pieces of chopped onion and lots of salt and pepper. The whole mass was well pressed down into the hot pan and then moved to a "medium" corner of the fire, there to remain for about half an hour. When the fishing had been unusually good and we needed no extra meat, the bacon was broken up in the potatoes just before we served them, otherwise it went

in between our buttered slices of bread. How good the ice-cold tomatoes with their spicy dressing tasted with the broiled fresh fish we basted with the bacon drippings, and how we argued over who should get the last crumb of brown potato before the pan was taken to the edge of the beach for its scrub with sand and sea water! Then big cups of strong black coffee and huge pieces of cake or pie and, while the sun set, someone stirred up the fire and a young voice started "Be My Little Baby Bumble Bee" or maybe a newer song like "By the Beautiful Sea." Is it any wonder I like HASHED BROWN POTATOES. But even without *my* memories, try them made just the same way on a prosaic stove. Let the boiled potatoes be cold and dry and have the bacon grease and skillet hot. For home consumption a few chopped onion tops or chives are better than the lustier sliced onion, and a dusting of chopped parsley makes them more delicate. The finished product, with some of our faithful poached eggs resting on top and the bacon curled about the edge, is a one-dish luncheon that any man, particularly, will relish. Sliced tomatoes in sharp dressing just like that made at the picnic, hot coffee, gingerbread from a good package mix, topped with marshmallows when it's half baked, fruit—and how long has it taken you? Not more than half an hour, including setting the table.

But you're not half through with those cold boiled potatoes when you've hashed browned them; no, indeed. Cut them into thick slices and make COUNTRY FRIES in a little bacon or chicken fat, with chopped parsley and salt just before you serve them.

For POTATOES AU GRATIN dice them, mix with about ¼ their amount of grated cheese, put them into a well-buttered casserole, cover with white sauce, dot with butter and crumbs, and bake for 20 minutes at 375°; or just heat them in the sauce with or without the cheese in the double boiler— that's a little quicker. For MACARONI AU GRATIN follow above.

Don't forget the recipe for potato salad (page 103) and if you have no mayonnaise or boiled dressing and no time to make it, lots of people like French dressing just as well on this dish, and any gourmet would prefer it to the bottled axle grease that masquerades as salad dressing on most grocery shelves. I have made this last taste almost homemade by the addition of vinegar, lemon juice, celery salt, cayenne, and a little mustard, but it's a thankless effort and takes almost as much time as whipping up a good dressing yourself.

An aspic jelly mix will produce TOMATO JELLY in little more that half an hour if you put it in individual moulds and in the coldest part of your icebox. Heat half the amount of tomato juice called for on the package to boiling, and dissolve the flavored gelatine thoroughly in it. Add the cool half of the juice, stir it well, then into the moulds and away to the freezer. One of the ever-handy hard-boiled eggs halved and put in the mould, cut side down, before the jelly goes in, makes this dressier, and if your pantry runs to a can of artichoke hearts, one of these is even better in the jelly, with half a stuffed egg—aren't they wonderful—on the side at serving time. A can of anchovies rolled or in long pieces won't set you back much and they are fine in salad or as a garnish on the aforementioned eggs in any style.

For a quick vegetable on the day when no cold boiled potatoes grace your icebox, try boiled BROAD NOODLES heaped in a dish with a generous dab of butter and a grating of cheese and bread crumbs on top. If neither the noodles nor the cooked potatoes are about don't be worried but cut up two or three cups of raw potatoes into small dice, dust them with flour, 1 tablespoon for each cup, add a few dabs of butter, put them in a shallow pan (the good old skillet again), cover them with top milk, and simmer carefully for 10 minutes. Then salt and pepper, and the ever useful chopped chives or parsley if handy, and TOP-OF-THE-STOVE SCALLOPED POTATOES is what you have.

Dinner, I admit, is harder to "emerge" than the simpler lunch, and if you have frequent unexpected guests for that meal the least nerve-wracking system is to have one or two menus that can be prepared with the help of the cans on your pantry shelves. A friend of mine calls creamed dried beef—the meat from a jar and evaporated milk in the sauce—waffles made with a biscuit mix, canned whole baby string beans, a salad, and hot gingerbread from a package, a "number one dinner," and a very good and filling one it is. A couple of jars of chicken à la king, touched up with sherry, would give a more elaborate air than the dried beef, but would likewise cost more. One of the canned luncheon meats like "Spam," left whole and glazed with the Virginia ham mix (page

157) of brown sugar and mustard, stuck with cloves and heated for 15 minutes, is another idea to keep in the back of your mind. Serve the sweet sour sauce (page 97) and canned mashed sweet potatoes in a casserole with this. Beat them up with a little butter and a few drops of sherry, season them well, and dot the tops with a few canned walnut halves before they go into the oven. Have canned tomatoes cooked down with a scraping of onion to go along.

The advent of the home freezer and the new refrigerators with a compartment for frozen foods is a real boon to the hostess with frequent unexpected guests, and we are just beginning to realize their potentialities. A frozen broiler or two, a package of corn, another of little green lima beans, the ever-present potatoes, creamed with parsley or fried, and for dessert a quart of ice cream right out of its hiding place on the cold shelf, with a sauce of strawberries from the same spot—a perfect menu and it's tucked away in an unbelievably small space.

A good first course for dinner or lunch in an emergency or otherwise is ANTIPASTO as the Italians serve it. It's a grand way to use up small amounts of leftover cooked vegetables, too. For each helping put a few leaves of lettuce on one of your prettiest salad plates, then a slice of tomato, half a hard-cooked egg (there I go again), cooked carrots, or a sliver or two of raw. The same goes for cauliflower, a stalk of celery, an anchovy or two or a sardine or a piece of tuna or salmon, a slice of bologna, ham or salami, spring onions, endive, any or all of these can go on the green. Pass the wine vinegar and a cruet of olive oil. It's not only delicious but lends a fillip to a dull meal that may have to follow after.

A young married couple I know take one night a week to "finish the refrigerator" and sit happily at the table surrounded by small dishes that look for all the world like the service in an old-time country hotel. That's not a bad way to get rid of leftovers, but antipasto seems much more subtle. The best way of all is to line up the remains of the last few meals and put your brains to work. One of our favorite dishes came from just such an effort and started with half of a cooked breaded veal cutlet, a few slices of fried eggplant, a saucer of string beans and a big dish of stewed tomatoes, all found in the icebox. I cut the veal and eggplant into narrow strips, put them in a casserole on top of a cupful of sliced onions previously softened in a little hot butter, poured the stewed tomatoes over all and baked it covered in a 375° oven for 45 minutes. Big potatoes went into the oven at the same time, and just before the casserole came out, the string beans were put in a circle on top of the meat and tomatoes. The result was so good that it was christened Veal à la Mama and is now a standard meal with us. It is just as delicious with leftover fried chicken, and cooked peas or asparagus tips are as good ingredients as the original string beans. You'll find the whole recipe on page 55.

Even my imagination was temporarily strained when six unexpected supper guests arrived at our house late one Sunday afternoon. Our own supper for two was to follow a heavy family midday dinner, and I hadn't given it much thought beyond being certain that there was enough cheese for a couple of sandwiches, a remnant of beefsteak, and half a cake about somewhere. All I could find to add to this was a head of lettuce, one big (fortunately) grapefruit, two oranges, half a lemon, a quart of milk and our six breakfast eggs. A frantic search brought to light one box of sardines tucked away on a shelf with my homemade pickles and jelly.

I often wonder why one of the numerous women's magazines does not run a cook's emergency contest to see just what can be produced with a minimum of material. Let's have our own contest now; so before you read further think for a minute what *you* would serve eight people with only those materials available. Allow yourself staples such as flour and coffee, and go to it.

Here's the meal I finally evolved. A platter at one end of the table was lined with the outside leaves of the lettuce and half filled with wafer thin slices of cold beefsteak, while the other half had sardines garnished with lemon slices. My biggest casserole almost overflowed with a cheese soufflé that was more milk, eggs and flour than cheese, but no one seemed to know the difference, and an equally large wooden bowl was heaped with lettuce, each leaf carefully torn and separated, in the midst of which a design of grapefruit and orange segments looked much more than it really was. Hot drop biscuits, dishes of jelly and my own pickles, and a big pot of coffee were on the table too, and by the time the guests came to the cake, which we almost had to divide with a slide rule, they were so full of what had the appearance, at least, of a big meal that the small piece seemed ample.

That hectic evening taught me a never-to-be-forgotten lesson and since then this has been my system, and a successful one I have found it. Plan one or two good simple meals for unexpected company and try to keep the ingredients for them always at hand, either in your icebox or on your pantry shelves. This is much better than a jumble of expensive trimmings crowding your storage space. When one item has been used up, fill its place immediately. Go into the fancy grocery department as far as your imagination and pocketbook will allow, but try to keep everything related. The price of a large jar of caviar or imported pâté de foie gras will stock your storeroom with what you need of canned tomatoes, string beans, Spam or a frozen chicken, and even leave enough for a can or two of anchovies and artichoke hearts.

Most of all, whether your emergency shelf and pocketbook allow you to start your meal with caviar and go on to tinned English pheasant, or whether, like most of us, you have to take a hurried look in the icebox to see what you can add to the eggs, try not to let those completely unexpected guests feel that you are embarrassed by their sudden appearance. Half the time they are a little embarrassed themselves. Keep cool, for both guests and hostess ill at ease hardly make for enjoyment, while a feeling all around the table of "Isn't this pot luck fun" gets any meal off to a good start.

MINIMUM EMERGENCY LIST

In the Refrigerator

Eggs, fresh and hard
    boiled
Boiled potatoes
½ lb bacon

Frozen chicken
Frozen corn
Frozen lima beans
Ice cream

(If your refrigerator has a place for them.) ←

In the Pantry

Canned string beans and/
    or asparagus
Canned tomatoes
Canned sweet potatoes
Spam
Deviled ham
Gingerbread mix

Evaporated milk
Grated cheese
Jellies
Pickles
Canned fruit
Favorite canned soups

Extras

Anchovies, whole and
    paste
Artichoke hearts
Tomato sauce
Tomato juice

Aspic-flavored gelatine
Sardines
Sharp cheese
and, Sh-h-h, maybe a jar
    of Caviar.

Painless Party Giving and Effortless Entertaining

To a hostess at home on the range, invited guests and their entertainment produce not only the thrill of a first-class parade but an appreciation of the Pennsylvania Dutch housewife's "Hard work to cook for less than ten, ain't?" since the best party menus are simply favorite family dishes with the quantities doubled or tripled. Certainly if your everyday food isn't good, what you serve your unfortunate guests won't be worth eating, either, and the relaxed mind that follows a lavish platter of some cheap but delicious stand-by is better than the jittery condition that too often accompanies a skimped expensive novelty that should first have been tried out on a patient husband and then had the directions written out.

These carefree standards of hospitality have had only one criticism that I can remember. That, coming from an alleged faithful female friend and being, "Of course, you're the only woman I know who could get away with party food like this," should be discounted, for her husband had just taken an enormous third helping of baked beans after a tremendous second one of cold meat loaf and salad, meantime inhaling beakers of coffee and keeping a watchful eye on the last doughnuts. Obviously he was making the most of his time before returning to an overpoweringly luxurious home, an irritable cook, and uninspired meals.

Buffet suppers are the most enjoyable method of entertaining in a simple household, and if you can get extra help, engage a dependable dishwasher. Otherwise rinse and stack the plates quickly and neatly, blithely facing next morning's early rising and cleaning up, for, helpful as they may wish to be, guests don't belong in the kitchen or pantry before or after a real party. Set the table and cook as far ahead as you can, and for easy service have two dishes of each food if you are entertaining more than eight. Pack away without regret your delicate china and banquet-size lace tablecloth, rout out extra card tables where your guests can eat in peace after they have filled their plates, and buy or make gay cotton covers and napkins which the laundry man can return unharmed. Purchase a couple of dozen cheap pottery plates—the mail order firms carry some beguiling designs—and start haunting secondhand shops for odd pieces of china or glass to add individuality to your table. You may have to go back perseveringly, time after time, to find just what you want but, oh, the sense of achievement when you run to ground just the set of sauce dishes or the compote you have yearned for! Patronize Ye Olde Antique Shoppe for these if your pocketbook allows, but why miss the thrill of the chase when what you save more than buys big and small wooden bowls and bright-colored tumblers from the five-and-ten.

My own favorite buffet table setting consists of four pottery soup tureens for the main dishes, big brown earthenware dinner plates, Mr. Woolworth's big and small wooden bowls for the salad, and cherry-red water glasses from the same emporium. The handleless coffee cups and their deep saucers are plain farmhouse white iron-stone, the dessert goes on small Pennsylvania Dutch pottery pie dishes of assorted patterns, and if cake is on the menu it very likely decorates the center of the table on a remarkable milk glass "hand" cake stand. A true junk-shop treasure and what a conversation piece. This whole mismatched service rests on a big brightly striped Guatemalan hammock that was brought me as a couch cover, is exceedingly good-looking, unusual, and what is even better, functional; and best of all, the whole outfit, eighteen of everything, cost less than $10. Perhaps instead of the hammock I cover the main table with an old-fashioned red-and-white cloth I picked up at a country store, or use as a centerpiece an ancient tin jelly mould or a funny white kitchen bowl filled with field flowers. The four squatty brass candlesticks at least look alike at first glance and their thorough yearly polishing, followed by a coat of clear nail polish, keeps them so gleaming that my guests don't notice how different each one really is.

Have lots of side dishes at your stand-up parties. It may be the old free-lunch influence but people do seem to enjoy being able to pick and choose. For that reason, curry makes one of the finest buffet suppers there is, and I've never found anyone who didn't enjoy its exotic flavor. Made with chicken, it is expensive, but cooked veal or pork can be used to eke out the bird, and cooked or canned shrimps are just as tasty. Curried hard-boiled eggs, perfect for a luncheon, don't seem quite enough for the main dish of a planned meal, but a big platter of cold meat loaf or cold cuts, with curried lentils at the other end of the table, is a fine, filling and cheap menu, especially if you don't forget the famous side dishes. Here is a typical menu for a curry supper:

Chicken curry and a separate dish of rice. Have some way of keeping them both hot at the table, or bring in just enough at once for one serving all round. Have plenty in reserve and be alert to replenish the containers before the first plate gets low. A salad of lettuce, tomatoes, radishes, cubes of cucumber, diced celery, and a few bits of dry crust that have been rubbed with garlic, all well tossed with an icy French dressing. Loaves of French or Italian bread, sliced diagonally halfway through, buttered, and warmed in the oven, or baskets of hot salt sticks and fresh rolls. Now for those side dishes. All of these are good. Grated peanuts—put them through the coarse cutter of the meat chopper. Chopped hard-boiled eggs. Slices of lime or lemon. Chopped onion. Chopped smoked ham or bacon. India relish or homemade green tomato pickle. Chutney (Major Grey's famous brand is best but our own is good, too) is a "must." Raisins. Grated fresh cocoanut. This is a job but worth the difference from the bought variety. Open the nut as gently as you can with a saw or hatchet—page the handyman—pry the nut from the shell, scrape off the brown outside and let the white chunks follow the peanuts through the meat chopper. Finally, Bombay Duck, which belies its name in being a rather smelly sun-dried fish imported from India in safely sealed tins. Big thin round cassava cakes that the Hindus toast and put under the rice come the same way and give an extra authentic touch. You can buy these at any shop which specializes in importing various unusual powders and spices. It was the late head of a famous Philadelphia firm himself, gazing at me sorrowfully over his steel-rimmed spectacles when I complained of the subdued flavor of his curry, who told me that he preferred not to have a mouth that felt like a bonfire after the first swallow, and always put just enough hot Nepal pepper (another specialty of the house) into his curry after it was served. He then presented me with a jar of their own particular brand of curry powder and benignly told me where to purchase a hotter variety. Whatever kind you use, put in a little at a time and let it cook a bit before you taste and add more. Any dish made with curry or chili powder is apt to get painfully hot very suddenly, and although it is simple to correct too mild a flavor, when it really burns your tongue not much can be done about it.

A chilled dry white wine, served in ice-filled highball glasses, with a dash of soda, goes well with this highly flavored meal and you will want a simple dessert afterwards. Perhaps big, black canned or fresh cherries, touched with brandy and poured over a mould of bought orange or lemon ice, or a well-chilled fruit compote and a light sponge cake.

One important help in keeping entertaining painless is to write down, as far ahead as possible, a complete menu of your planned meal. And by complete, I mean really complete. Not just chicken, rice, salad, dessert. Do it on a large sheet of paper divided into three columns. Write the proposed menu in one column, and what is on hand and the necessary marketing in the other two. For example, the list for the curry supper I have suggested might look like this:

MENU	ON HAND	ORDER
Martinis	Vermouth	Gin
Olives	Olives	½ lb Roquefort
Cheese Pâté	Lemons	1 cream cheese
	Chives	Sherry
Curried chicken	Onions	2–6 lb stewing chickens
		1 bunch celery
		2 large apples
Rice	Rice	—
Salad	Tomatoes	2 heads lettuce
	Vinegar	2 bunches radishes
		1 cucumber
		olive oil
French bread	Butter	2 loaves French bread (if none, yeast cake for rolls)

Side dishes:

MENU	ON HAND	ORDER
India relish	India relish	—
Cocoanut	—	1 cocoanut

Side dishes (cont.):

Hard-boiled eggs	Eggs	—
Chutney	Chutney Onions	—
Chopped ham	—	½ lb cooked ham or bacon
Chopped onion	Onions	—
Peanuts	—	½ lb salted peanuts
Sliced limes	—	½ dozen limes
Bombay Duck	—	1 tin Bombay Duck
Fruit compote	Oranges	2 grapefruit 1 fresh pineapple 1 lb Belgian grapes 1 box fresh or frozen strawberries
Sponge cake	All materials	—
Coffee	Coffee	—
Wine	—	1 small peach brandy 2 bottles wine
Soda	—	6 bottles soda
Coca-Cola	Coca-Cola	—
Beer	—	1 case beer

Do your marketing clutching the list in your hand, and if you are unable to get any particular item, cross off the original and write down the replacement. This done, tear off the menu and hang it up in the kitchen where you can keep an eye on it. All this may seem an effort but once you get in the habit you'll no longer be discouraged by finding a forgotten plate of appetizers in the icebox long after your guests have departed. For overnight or longer-staying visitors, the same written menus are invaluable. Plan and do the ordering as far ahead as you can, write everything down, and you'll be saved that "what am I going to give them for lunch?" sensation that otherwise comes like a blow on the head just as breakfast has been cleared away.

As for people who go in for elaborate lists of what they last fed a given group of friends, or what is equally dull, notes on their guests' likes or dislikes in food, phooie, say I. Any hostess worth her salt should be able to remember what her friends can't or won't eat, and as for the things they do like, show me the woman, or particularly the man, who isn't able to go to town with a favorite food almost indefinitely, while specialties of the house are always looked forward to, no matter how many times they have been served before.

Now back to our CHICKEN CURRY. For twelve people cover 2 cut-up, 5 or 6-pound stewing chickens with cold water. Add 2 peeled chopped onions, ½ cup of celery leaves, and a few sprigs of parsley. Simmer, keeping the meat well covered with water, until it is tender, which only you can tell for it depends on the age and innocence of the bird itself. Start testing it with a fork and add salt to taste after the first 45 minutes. When the fork goes into a drumstick easily, the bird is done. Drain the meat and let it and the broth cool, then remove the skin and cut the chicken into good-sized pieces. No delicate mincing here, this is a sturdy dish. Skim the fat from the broth and put 6 tablespoons of it into a saucepan—a large one for this is going to be the future home of your entire dish—set it over a medium fire, and add 2 cups of chopped peeled white onions, 1 cup of chopped celery, and 2 chopped tart apples that have been peeled and cored. This last is not absolutely necessary, but it does add a certain flavor. Cover and let them simmer until the onions are soft and starting to color. Add the cut-up chicken and enough broth, measuring it as it goes in, to more than cover the meat, say 2 inches above, for you want plenty of sauce. If there isn't enough broth, add water or half-and-half canned consommé and water. Let things come to a boil and then for every cup of liquid stir in slowly ½ teaspoon of curry powder and ½ tablespoon of flour that have been blended to a smooth paste with plenty of cold water. Simmer it gently for 15 or 20 minutes, taste it for flavor, and add salt or curry powder if you think they are needed. If the sauce seems thin, thicken it with cornstarch dissolved in cold water. Put this in, a little at a time, and let the chicken boil up well after each addition. The finished sauce should be thinner than the usual gravy, yet it should have quite a bit of body. Let it simmer 15 minutes longer. Give it a final taste for seasoning and it's ready to serve or better still to rest in the icebox overnight, well covered, to let its flavor blend before reheating. Then bring on the boiled rice and trimmings, and when you serve the curry don't forget to supply your guests with a dessert spoon in addition to the usual fork. That's the way it's done in India and the extra utensil is a great help in getting those delicious last juicy bits off the plate. The same sauce made with chicken broth or half canned consommé and half water can be used for cooked meat, shrimps or eggs. Add any leftover meat gravy before the flour and curry powder.

CURRIED LENTILS or "DAH" is a domesticated East Indian dish taught me by that famous Baltimore hostess, Mrs. William Bevan, and worthy of her. For twelve people: Soak 2 cups of lentils overnight. Next morning drain and cook them in 8 cups of seasoned chicken broth or the diluted canned consommé until tender, about 1 hour. Drain and save the stock you have cooked them in. Stir 2 cups of sliced onions on a medium fire in 4 tablespoons of butter until very tender but not browned. Add the lentils, 2 tablespoons of curry powder, 2 tablespoons of lime juice, mix well, and then put in just enough of the stock to make a dish that can be easily "spooned out." Another recipe that takes to an overnight rest and reheating in a double boiler and enjoys chutney and the other curry accompaniments. Any leftover can be put through a sieve and added to the remaining stock for a delicious soup.

I never prepare rice without remembering my first experience with that expanding grain. I had promised my just-married husband his favorite stewed chicken and rice and, making the usual stop at his club before dinner, such was his pride in my cooking that every time he boasted of his coming meal he felt forced to invite one more hungry bachelor to share it. As each phone call announced an extra guest I made more gravy and lightheartedly measured out another cupful of rice, then filled what seemed an adequate pot with water and started cooking it. Soon to my shocked surprise I was frantically hurling the cereal into bigger and bigger containers with more and more water, and, I don't wonder now that roars of laughter greeted the hysterical bride who was discovered wringing her hands while gazing with wide-eyed horror at a large dishpan heaped full of boiled rice. With this cautionary tale in mind, remember that one cup of uncooked rice will, after treatment, feed three, and for our curry supper for twelve take four cups, put it in a sieve, and wash it well under running cold water to completely free each grain from its starch covering. Have a big pot filled with boiling water, add 1 tablespoon of salt for each quart of the liquid, and then add the rice so slowly that the bubbling never ceases. When the last of the rice is in, give the pot one quick thorough stir down to the bottom and let the boiling continue without any more disturbance. At the end of 15 minutes test to see if it's done, and if you have allowed the rice to dry thoroughly after its cold bath it shouldn't take longer than that. When a grain pressed between thumb and finger feels tender all the way through, take the rice off the stove, put it in a colander or large sieve, run more cold water through it and return it in the sieve to the stove for 10 minutes to regain its heat over a little hot water. It can be put in a medium oven for this if you prefer, and if it has to be kept waiting, remember that it is much more palatable cooked just enough and on the cool side than as a hot but overdone gluey mass. What goes over the rice is the article that must be kept at top temperature.

FRUIT COMPOTE is the perfect dessert to follow a rich meal and for twelve people buy 1 fresh pineapple, or use 6 slices of the canned variety. Core and remove the rind of the fresh fruit and cut it or the canned slices into inch cubes. Add the segments of 2 large grapefruit and 4 good-sized oranges, and a pint box of hulled and washed strawberries, or the same amount of frozen ones, with a squeeze of lime or lemon juice. Melt ½ cup of sugar in ½ cup of warm water and sweeten the fruit lightly with this. Arrange the fruit tastefully in your prettiest glass bowl, pour over it a half-cup or maybe more of the best peach or apricot brandy you can buy. Put it in the icebox to chill and when it comes on the table watch your guests sniff appreciatively as they help themselves.

The college football season and the late return from the games through the crisp fall evening always seemed to call for at least one fish chowder party with the soup steaming in my grandmother's big tureen, plenty of warm pilot biscuits, a big bowl of tart cole slaw, side dishes of pickled beets, mustard pickle and pickled peaches, and for dessert hot baked apple dumplings, cheese and thick cream. Sometimes there was a plate of doughnuts to dunk in the coffee, and on really chilly nights a crock of homemade baked beans and a cruet of tomato catsup followed the chowder. A menu that can be prepared ahead and is guaranteed to thaw a frozen group in record time.

Make the FISH CHOWDER (for twelve again) this way: Buy six pounds of codfish or haddock. Have the fishman skin and bone it, and take the trimmings and two or three fish heads home with the fish. Put the trimmings and heads into a saucepan, add ½ cup of chopped celery and the same of onion, a sprig of parsley, a small piece of bay leaf, and a few whole peppercorns. Cover with 2 quarts of water and let it simmer for 1 hour. Strain out the bones etc., and you have the rich fish stock that chefs call *court bouillon*. Cut 1 pound of fat salt pork with the rind removed into small dice and fry them in a deep pot until crisp and brown. Add 4 cups of chopped onions and cook 3 minutes more. Now add the fish, cut up into good-sized pieces, and 4 cups of diced white potatoes. Cover this with 8 cups of fish stock, making up any difference with water, pop on the lid, and let everything simmer 20 minutes until the potatoes and onions are tender. In another pot melt ½ cup of butter and blend into it ¾ cup of flour. Stir in slowly 2 quarts of milk, add salt to taste and a good twist of the pepper grinder, and simmer for 15 minutes. When you're ready to serve the chowder, combine the contents of the two pots, bring it to a quick boil for 5 minutes, and when it comes to the table let it wear a few yellow bits of melting butter and a frost of paprika and chopped parsley. Have big deep bowls, not shallow soup plates, to eat it from and put a warm pilot biscuit in the bottom of each before you ladle out the soup. If pilot biscuit or "sea toast" isn't available soda crackers make an acceptable substitute. This soup is apt to curdle if kept hot indefinitely, but both parts can be made ahead and reheated before mixing together.

Many of my recipes have a history and baked beans always bring back the Maine woods and the lovely camp that a friend of ours owned on a lake there. Before the summer season and real style arrived, the place was cared for by John, the general factotum, and his wife, Mollie, whose baked beans were deservedly famous. She wrote down her recipe for me one cool June evening, and while she was explaining that the touch of ginger was what made it outstanding, the men were questioning John on the winter's gossip in the small nearby town. "Well," said John, "about the only thing that's happened is that George Brown's youngest daughter is in trouble on account of that feller that's been boarding with her folks." "I guess George didn't like that too much," someone put in. John thought a moment and then came out with the typical Maine understatement that has been a byword in our house ever since. "George was pretty dam' mad for about an hour," he said.

Here's the recipe for BAKED BEANS. I cook them in a big brown lidded crock and generally serve them in that, too, but for a change put them in a shallow glass baking dish after cooking and let them get a rich brown again in a hot oven before they go to the table. Take your choice of service but don't forget Mollie's advice to deal gently with the ginger. Wash and pick over 1 quart of big white pea beans and soak them overnight in three times their quantity of water. Next morning drain the beans, cover them with fresh water, and simmer slowly until a few picked up in a spoon will burst their skins when you blow gently on them. A remarkable direction, I grant, but the only satisfactory method. While the beans are cooking, scrape the rind of a ¾-pound piece of salt pork, cut it into 3 pieces, and let it stand in boiling water for a few minutes. In the bottom of your bean pot put one small peeled onion and a piece of pork. Half fill with the drained beans and add another onion and piece of pork. Fill the pot to within 2 inches of the top, bury one more onion just below the surface of the beans, and add the remaining piece of pork with its rind just showing. Mix 1 tablespoon of salt, 1 teaspoon of dry mustard, and ¼ teaspoon of ground ginger with 2 cups of the water the beans were boiled in. Stir in 1 cup of New Orleans molasses and ½ cup of tomato catsup and pour over the beans, adding enough of the bean water to fill the pot. Put on the lid and bake in a very slow oven (275°) for at least 6 hours, and preferably overnight. Peek at them every two hours or so to see that the water hasn't cooked away, add more if necessary, and if they are to cook while you sleep, be sure that the liquid comes well up under the lid before you leave them. Let them brown, uncovered, for half an hour before serving, and if you're planning on reheating and serving from the crock, allow at least 45 minutes in a 300° oven for them to get hot all through again, keeping the lid on and not letting the liquid get below the beans.

Cole slaw (page 102) for our hungry twelve will take 3 quarts of finely chopped cabbage and double one of the recipes for boiled dressing (page 102). Let it chill thoroughly and after you put it in the big wooden bowl decorate its edges with quartered tomatoes if you wish, though this homely meal hardly calls for trimmings.

The apples for the dumplings can be peeled, cored and left covered with cold water to which has been added a little lemon juice and salt, but they mustn't wait too long, and APPLE DUMPLINGS are really better made ahead and reheated. Put 1 tablespoon of brown sugar (or more if the fruit is sour) and ½ teaspoon of butter and a dash of nutmeg in the center of each apple. Roll out thin 6-inch squares of piecrust (page 117) for each one. Fold the corners of the crust over the top of the apple, pinch the sides together and bake on a greased pan in a 350° oven for 45 minutes. Pass the cream and sugar with these. Ice-cold beer goes well with this meal and don't forget the always welcome coffee.

Although there have been those who wondered how, what with the constant riot and number of guests of all ages continually under foot in their home, our offspring ever had the time and privacy in which to make or receive a proposal, both the children married young. When the second wedding approached we put up a brave front, but both my husband and I were sure that with the fledglings gone the old nest was going to be a grim place. A feeling which was encouraged by certain of our more settled friends who broadly hinted that a frustrated desire for peace and quiet might be the answer to this family epidemic of early matrimony. To our delight we never got time to oil up the wheelchairs to which we had threatened to retire, for the last confetti and rice were hardly cleared away before the children and their friends were back, and even if our house seemed a bit empty in the day and late at night, dinnertime was as gay and noisy as ever.

Sunday was the real evening for a home reunion and my contention that a good dish never palls was vindicated, for every week the same crowd ate chili and to a man—and girl—appeared the next Sunday ready to tackle another round of the identical food. At rare intervals I switched to Spanish rice. Once I remember we had spaghetti and a flag-draped transparency (made of white shelf paper) over the door said sadly in large crayon letters "A Reverdici Giuseppe Jonesetti" for war was in the air and the first of the lads to go maintained that his group at training camp was chiefly Italian. But CHILI was the real Sunday favorite and needless to say I liked it, too, because it could be prepared the Saturday or even Friday before. Here is how I did it, and again twelve seemed to be the right number to look forward to serving. Have the butcher grind 2½ pounds of top of the round, or do it yourself, but don't, I beg again, buy ready-ground "hamburg." Melt 4 tablespoons of butter in a big saucepan, put in the meat, 6 cups of coarsely chopped onions and 2 chopped cloves of garlic. Cover and let it simmer for 30 minutes, stirring well from the bottom once in a while. Then add 4 cans of kidney beans and 3 cans of tomatoes, salt and pepper to taste, and 3 teaspoons of chili powder, always heeding the warning to go slowly at first with a hot seasoning, adding more later if needed. Let it all just simmer 2 hours and for the last half of that time you will have to watch and stir it fairly frequently lest it scorch. This is really the main buffet dish par excellence. It is delicious, filling, can be made ahead, and if you supply yourself with extra cans of tomatoes and beans the unexpected famished guest can cause no worries. Just dump in sufficient more tomatoes and beans, give them a few minutes to boil up, and while the chili may not be so meaty it will still be very appetizing. Serve cornbread made from a mix, with this. Follow the directions on the package, bake it in thin layers in round cake pans, and keep it coming out of the oven; cut in wedge-shaped pieces. The salad bowl might hold finely chopped celery, bits of hard-boiled egg, and a few cans of anchovies, mixed with its lettuce and French dressing (page 100), and for dessert how about home-canned or brandied peaches (page 133)? A cake, too, if your company is still at that happy calory-unconscious age. Coffee and dry red wine are as good with this meal as with spaghetti, although I have found that youth prefers, and is doubtless better off with the plebeian beer.

This recipe for SPANISH RICE will serve eight. Heat 6 tablespoons of olive oil until it crackles—no substitutes here for you need the flavor of the real McCoy. Add 3 cups of washed rice, 2 cups of coarsely chopped onions, 1 chopped garlic clove, 2 shredded green peppers (seeds and white pulp removed), and an optional cup of sliced mushrooms, and stir over a hot fire until the rice starts to pop and brown and the vegetables are soft, about 15 minutes. Put in a deep casserole, allowing enough room for the rice to swell to four times its bulk. Add 2 cans of tomatoes, 2 cans of condensed consommé, and season with salt and pepper. Stir well. Cover the casserole tightly and cook in a 350° oven for 1 hour. Do not stir again. Look at it when half done and add 1 cup of consommé if it seems dry, for rice does vary in its absorptive qualities. Serve in the casserole in which it was baked, and pass grated Italian cheese. Sliced Italian ham goes well with this, or have plates of antipasto ready on the table as a first course, and you'll need nothing else except the warmed, already buttered bread, and coffee.

I usually make my SPAGHETTI WITH MEAT for a more filling dish, although without the meat the sauce itself is delicious. For twelve, take 1 pound of ground top of the round, season with salt, pepper, and ½ cup of chopped parsley, and form into small balls the size of marbles. Brown these with an optional cup of sliced mushrooms in 4 tablespoons of butter. Cover and keep warm. The SPAGHETTI SAUCE is simplicity itself. Soften 1 cup of finely chopped onions and 2 chopped garlic cloves in 4 tablespoons of olive oil. Add 2 cans of tomatoes, 2 cans of condensed consommé and 2 cans of tomato paste. The Italian variety that is labeled *con basilico* is best. Each can contains a leaf of sweet basil, and if you are unable to find the brand, put in a pinch of the dried herb. Simmer the sauce 15 minutes, stirring constantly, strain it through a sieve, and keep it hot. Cook 1 pound of spaghetti in boiling salted water 10 minutes, if you want what Italians call *a la dente,* meaning chewy, and 5 minutes longer if you like it soft. Drain and return to the stove over hot water. Serve with the small meat balls and their juice over it, and have the hot tomato sauce and grated cheese in separate dishes.

Our last summer cottage was in a deserted and most unexclusive but cheap section of the coast. Its 2½ bedrooms hardly held all of us, and though really a completely self-sufficient family we do love company. This lack was soon remedied by the discovery in the general store of a fly-specked dozen of picture postals which, though they gave our house the appearance of a Hollywood palace, at least showed how to reach it. We marked our villa with the usual cross, wrote on the message side over our name "Clam Chowder, Beer, Sandwiches and Swimming Every Sunday After Twelve. Guests Please Bring Their Own Bath Towels," addressed them to friends, and let Uncle Sam do the rest. The results threatened to be overwhelming, but the whole family took turns grinding clams on Saturday afternoons, and Sunday mornings, with everything under control, we'd bet on who and how many would appear that particular day. The CLAM CHOWDER was the Manhattan variety, sniffed at by all true New Englanders, but their creamy style will curdle when kept hot and this won't. This will serve twelve: Scrub 4 dozen large chowder clams (quahogs) and put them in a big covered pot with 2 cups of boiling water. Let them steam until just opened. Remove the clams, pry open the shells, and take out the meat. Strain and reserve the juice in the pot. Grind the clams coarsely, strain and mix the juices. Remove the rind from 1 pound of fat salt pork, cut it into small dice, and fry until crisp in a large pot. Then add 2 cups of chopped onions and cook 5 minutes. Add 2 cups of diced potatoes, 5 cups of the clam juice (eked out with water if necessary), 1 cup of diced carrots, the same of chopped celery, and 8 cups of canned tomatoes. Season with 1 teaspoon of thyme and ½ teaspoon of pepper. Boil 15 minutes, add the chopped clams, and boil for 15 minutes more.

Our open-faced BATHING SUIT SANDWICHES were deservedly famous that summer. These have as a foundation a buttered slice of pumpernickel or rye bread cut crosswise from a round loaf. On this go layers of lettuce, sliced tomatoes, onion rings, and anchovies, with hand-ground black pepper and a little anchovy oil on top. Needless to say, they are best eaten on a sunny beach with a bottle of cold beer frosting on the sand nearby, but a knife and fork will housebreak them to a degree. SUBMARINE SANDWICHES are a close relation, a little better trained, perhaps, but just as hunger-appeasing. Split and butter long Italian or French rolls and fill them with lettuce, sliced tomatoes, onion rings, sliced Italian salami, and slivers of Provalona or Swiss cheese. A little olive oil, and just a touch of hot Italian red pepper finishes these before they receive their covers. Have the makings and rolls on the table and let the guests, as the family says, loom up their own.

The chowder, beer and sandwiches were served, before or after swims, and we sped our guests with hot coffee and cinnamon bun. This last was often bought, to my shame, but procuring, opening and grinding the clams took almost all Saturday and to really cook for a crowd on summer Sundays is too much to ask.

In the days when that evening bore the blessed title "cook's night out," every Thursday all one winter was "milk toast night," too. It started when a friend dropped in on my husband, who had been advised to stick to a light diet for a few days, and said he also liked the nursery dish. It may have been nostalgia for a lost youth that seems to affect so many of our generation, but a surprising number of guests began appearing and extra milk and cream on Thursday, with a baking of bread on Wednesday, became the rule.

The "setting" was a toaster at each end of the table and a bowl and spoon for each guest—period! The "menu"—plenty of half-and-half milk and cream kept hot in a double boiler, 2 loaves of bread, a dish of butter, salt, pepper, and a castor of flavored salts—garlic, onion, and the like—was an equally effortless preparation. Each guest sliced his bread and adjusted the toaster to his liking and the arguments that went on as to whether the true gourmet preferred light or dark toast, eaten crisp, or after softening with milk, the amount of butter, and the best mixtures of seasonings, would have done credit to a meeting of a wine and food society. Sure proof that the simplest food can make a "party" for congenial folk.

Here is a list of further main dishes that are all excellent for buffet suppers, with the references to the recipes for preparing them. Increase the quantities as necessary:

Virginia ham . . . . pg. 157
Meat loaf . . . . pg. 53
Deviled mutton. . . . . pg. 50
Crab Imperial . . . . pg. 80
Shrimp Florentine . . . . pg. 80
Scalloped oysters. . . . . pg. 76
Chicken Cacciatore . . . . pg. 51
Lamb stew . . . . pg. 55
Beef and Kidney pie . . . . pg. 56
Veal and Ham pie. . . . . pg. 57
Deviled clams . . . . pg. 77
Salmon mousse. . . . . pg. 79

Decorations for the table, and entertainment after the guests have enjoyed a well-cooked meal should go right along with the careful beforehand planning of the menu, for like a well-arranged parsley or watercress garnish they add the perfect finishing touch.

Thank heaven the time has gone when bunches of stiff expensive flowers cut off from view the other side of the table. A few blooms in a low container are easier on our modern eyes, and with all the books that are available on simple flower arrangement even the most unskilled nongarden-clubber ought to be able to achieve an attractive result. Snoop around secondhand shops for odd and unusual "vases," my pride in this connection being a brown Bennington kitchen soap dish. It cost twenty-five cents but, filled with colorful flowers, it elicits comment far above its lowly origin. Keep an eye out for odd bits of silvery Britannia ware too. Dull their surfaces may be in the dusty shop but if the lines are good an inexpensive replating will restore the finish, and an ancient metal spoon holder trailing the sheen of ivy is much more charming for a simple informal table decoration than all the orchids the florist could supply. Marigolds, zinnias, petunias, and many other flowers are easily raised from seed and a place should be kept in the smallest garden for these never-failing friends of the dining-room table.

Let the younger members of the family join in holiday preparation. We looked forward to helping grandmother stuff the Christmas turkey just as much as hanging up our stockings, and "putting in the stuff" is still an eagerly awaited moment for my own grandchildren. In most homes there exist equally pleasant traditions that should never be allowed to lapse. But besides the big holidays don't forget the many less important ones that can be turned into a "party" too, if only by serving Irish stew or green frosted cake on St. Patrick's Day or passing hatchet-shaped cookies with the Twenty-second of February dessert.

When our daughter-in-law to be first appeared for family dinner after her engagement, we had a flower-bedecked rather gruesome glove form sporting a tremendous gleaming "diamond," on the proper finger, in the center of the table, and she still cherishes it.

Mother's Day with its bathos is always a field day for our unsentimental family and their prize effort was undoubtedly sneaking into the house a readymade cake on which a surprised Whistler's "Mother," looking as though she had had a hard night, was startlingly depicted in chocolate icing. A close second was when, after my always ill-tempered week of putting away winter clothes, a May Sunday morning found the hall ceiling trailing a huge sheet banner on which remarkable winged creatures gamboled amidst the letters of "Moth-er, we love you!"

Father's Day calls for equal celebration, and the man in question having supposedly lurid taste in clothing, his gifts of dime-store lightning-struck neckties and passion-flowered shorts, not to mention campaign buttons bearing more or less disrespectful filial sentiments, would undoubtedly call forth a record outburst from the head of the family in Clarence Day's play.

Try the oft-repeated and not difficult admonition to remember the birthdays and anniversaries of your friends. It's a worthwhile effort and a calendar kept up to date and consulted every so often helps. A sudden shower of unexpected gifts may embarrass the recipient, but a candlelit homemade cake appearing at the end of a meal, with just one package, can never fail to touch his or her heart. The same cake, topped by small figures of bride and groom bought from a baker, will charm an old or newly married pair. On these occasions, something inexpensive but funny or appropriate, produced from its hiding place at the right moment, calls forth laughter and appreciation that a hurriedly purchased or expensive gift may miss.

An engaged couple and their wedding party will enjoy mixing the wedding cake after a buffet supper much more than taking part in just another "shower." Arrange with the local caterer for the baking and have ready beforehand the measured but not prepared ingredients for a fruitcake (page 114). After the table has been cleared cover it, and the floor too, with newspapers or clean dustcloths. Give each guest an apron—these may be souvenirs or your own kitchen coveralls—and let them all go to work by pairs on a prearranged schedule of beating eggs, slicing citron, and sorting raisins and currants. When everything is done the helpers should assist in the mixing, with the bride and groom giving a last stirring "for luck." Next morning take the batter to be baked in one large and one smaller layer, and give the date of the wedding so that it can be iced and delivered on that day, with the formal bridal figures placed on the summit of the pyramid. Some sentimental brides like to serve only the larger bottom cake to their wedding guests, and have the smaller one well wrapped after the reception to be saved for their first anniversary. This party can be given long before those usually hectic weeks immediately preceding the wedding, for once baked the cake is better the longer it is kept. Your dining room may appear a mild shambles after the mixing party, but their enjoyment at the moment and the interest and professional pride the amateur caterers show later when the imposing tower of cake finally greets their eyes is worth a few crushed raisins on an easily cleaned rug.

In the same mood is a plum-pudding party, with all hands after supper helping to prepare their share of the holiday specialty. Use the recipe on page 116.

The real secret of successful after-dinner entertainment lies in the careful choosing, beforehand, of congenial guests. Not necessarily all close friends, for a few strangers add spice to any group, but serious bridge players hardly relish being forced to join in wild seven-card stud poker. And the couple whose idea of a good evening is a rousing ping pong tournament won't enjoy the sedate pencil and paper games of the intelligentsia. Any party goes better if the implements for the evening's entertainment quietly appear before the after-dinner lull sets in and conversation reaches too dull a level. Of course, there are plenty of people who really like to talk all night, and these blessed groups rate having the evening refreshments, be they highballs, beer or Coca-Cola, brought out a little early, for in helping the flow of thought a tinkling glass, like a bird, in the hand is worth two somewhere else.

Household crises can be taken in stride and turned to advantage, too, as witness the farewell spur-of-the-minute picnic, long remembered by those who attended, that took place in our empty house when we were about to move to another city. Packing cases were the chairs and tables, and the hilarious meal was served on paper plates and cups after being cooked in the fireplace. And perhaps our most successful party was the direct result of a hard-hearted paperhanger's refusal to change the appointed date for doing over our first floor. The necessity of clearing the grimy walls of their camouflage of pictures didn't leave rooms that looked at all prepared for entertaining, and out-of-town friends were due for a suddenly announced but long-awaited visit. Unconcerned, we presented each guest after dinner with a large package of colored crayons and allowed them to satisfy the wicked urge that we all have to deface a blank surface. Even next morning's early rising to forestall the paperhanger's crew and erase some of the more realistic efforts couldn't spoil the memory of twelve supposedly grown-up, settled people having a completely uninhibited and uproarious evening.

Give Your Friends a
Break with Breakfasts

hen next about to ask your favorite friends for dinner, hesitate
and listen instead to the extra enthusiastic acceptance that follows an invitation to Sunday breakfast *en negligé*. Somewhere
between ten and eleven is a good hour to set, as it gives everyone, including
the hostess, time for a weekend sleep yet doesn't interfere with possible afternoon engagements. Out-of-towners and those unfortunate folk who must
live in hotels particularly appreciate a glimpse of family life on a Sunday and
if you order their home-town paper delivered with your own, their gratitude
for such thoughtfulness is likely to be overwhelming. And be sure to be lavish with the coffee for that wonderful relaxed moment when, replete with
food, surrounded by a fog of cigarette smoke, and snowed under by the
comic and sport sections, everyone wants the second or third cup that there
isn't time to sip leisurely on a hurried weekday morning.

Start off with lots of ice-cold fruit or vegetable juice, not neglecting
such delicacies as peaches or strawberries when they are in season, and for a
small number it's fun and easy to have next a big choice of the cold cereals

that come so tidily packaged in individual boxes. On a cold winter morning watch your guests make a sheepish but willing "just this once" exception in favor of fattening hot oatmeal.

The conventional eggs and bacon with toast are always acceptable but let's have a little more heartwarming main course to celebrate the day when no one has to hurry off to train or office. Perhaps SAUSAGE, in links or cakes, fried for 10 minutes over a hot fire and then drained of the grease and given 20 minutes in a 375° oven, or SCRAPPLE, now that the famous Philadelphia dish has wandered from its native heath in cans. The traditional and only way to achieve a perfect result with this no longer local food is to start thick slices cooking in a cold pan over a medium heat. Fry each side 10 or 15 minutes until a crisp rich brown, let no foreign coating of flour, batter or crumbs sully its original purity, and turn each piece only once. Follow these directions closely and William Penn's reproachful ghost will never haunt you.

Renowned in song and story as scrapple is, when the City of Brotherly Love really relaxes on a Sunday morning the table is more than likely to groan under a great dish of steaming KIDNEY STEW, rightly considered a very different article indeed from the dull "stewed kidney" that other districts offer. One of my ancient cookbooks speaks of always demanding a "nice, fresh beef kidney" for this, leaving the cook with the idea that an impertinent but kindly bull should be just around the corner, ready for the sacrifice, but a local butcher is sure to provide you satisfactorily with the 1 large or 2 small ones you need for four people, without your having to delve into the original owner's disposition or home life. Use a pot of ample size, cover the meat with cold water, and bring slowly to a boil. Simmer for 15 minutes. Drain off the water and wash the pot and the kidney, too. Cover the kidney again with cold water, add 1 chopped onion, 2 tablespoons of chopped celery or celery tops, and a sprig of parsley. Let it simmer until the kidney is so tender that a fork will pierce it easily; about 6 hours, or overnight, if you have a controllable stove, is better. Long slow cooking does it and it must be kept below boiling. As you remove it from the stove add 1 teaspoon of salt, and let it cool in the water in which it was cooked. When ready to proceed remove the fat and strain and reserve the water. Chip the kidney into pieces about the size of a thick five-cent piece and, if you have done a good job of simmering it slowly, there should be very little tough core to discard. Melt 3 tablespoons of kidney fat or butter in a saucepan, add 2 tablespoons of flour, and when it bubbles add slowly 3 cups of the water in which the kidney was boiled. Let this simmer 10 minutes, then add the kidney and 2 chopped hard-boiled eggs. After another 10 minutes simmering, if the gravy does not seem quite thick enough, add a bit of cornstarch dissolved in cold water, a very little at a time. Taste it for salt, add more if needed, with a dash of cayenne and black pepper. Just before serving stir in 1 teaspoon of Worcestershire sauce and 1 tablespoon of sherry, and have both these condiments and cayenne pepper too, on the table. Prepared as above, this is guaranteed to make any exiled Friend burst into nostalgic tears, and I know one homesick lad who attempted its manufacture on a collapsible stove in a foreign pension!

CODFISH CAKES shouldn't belong only on a Boston breakfast table and now that it is no longer necessary to soak, shred and pick the fish ourselves they are a joy to make. For four people, run cold water through 1 cup of already shredded, packaged fish that has been placed in a fine sieve, and press very dry. Add to this 1 well-beaten egg and beat together. Beat in 2 cups of hot mashed or riced potatoes and ⅛ teaspoon of black pepper, and let it cool a little before you form it into round flat cakes or balls. The balls will have to be fried in deep hot fat but the cakes do very well cooked in ½ inch of grease in a skillet on a medium fire. Bacon fat is good for this and so are bacon strips as a garnish. Spicy homemade tomato catsup (page 129) and doughnuts (page 144) should accompany this for real New Englanders, but let's pass up the Northern cold breakfast pie.

Boiled rock fish (page 78) is another different breakfast dish, and CREAMED FINNAN HADDIE too rarely makes a morning appearance in this part of the English-speaking world. For four, cover a 2½-pound piece of finnan haddie with half-and-half milk and water, bring to a slow boil, and simmer for 25 minutes. Drain and place on a hot platter, cover it with 2 cups of white sauce (page 94), and sprinkle with chopped parsley.

Pan-broiled shad roe and crisp strips of bacon wreathed with shining green watercress and red radishes and accompanied by fried tomatoes make a spring breakfast straight from heaven. Expensive, too, as most heavenly things are. Imagine my indignation when two visiting Californians announced that they considered the delicate fish eggs an overrated Eastern specialty. California, there they went! The tomatoes are on page 86, and SHAD ROE for four calls for 1 or 2 sets of roe gently poached for 15 minutes in salted water to cover. Add 1 tablespoon of vinegar to keep the roe light-colored and firm. Drain the fragile things carefully. Fry 6 pieces of bacon and reserve. Have the bacon grease hot and carefully ease in the roe, for it's vicious stuff when cooking and hisses and spits like a snake. Cook 10 minutes on each side on a medium hot stove, then onto a warm platter with the bacon, to acquire its garland of green and red. Don't forget, when fresh or canned roe means just a pain in the pocketbook, that the fried tomatoes and bacon make a fine breakfast in their own right.

My father-in-law, a famous amateur chef, used to like to prepare CREAMED DRIED BEEF and hot cakes for his Sunday breakfast. For four these were his directions for what he called "frizzled beef." Shred ¼ pound of dried beef. Melt ¼ cup of butter with ½ cup of water and a scrape of onion in a skillet, add the beef and stir over a medium hot fire. When the water cooks away and the meat starts to brown and "frizzle," which means "curl" in these degenerate days of perfect permanent waves, scrape it to the side of the pan and in the empty space shake 1½ tablespoons of flour. Slowly stir in 2 cups of cream or top milk, and simmer 5 minutes longer.

These main dishes, although complete in themselves, do yearn for waffles or hot cakes as side partners, especially on a Sunday, and that lack is easiest supplied by using one of the bought "mixes" which are simple to make and foolproof when the directions are followed. Waffles can be cooked and served at the table, thanks to Mr. Edison, but unfortunately most people consider three or four hot cakes just a single helping and the electric griddle, fitted with a belt conveyor, that will produce them in that profusion hasn't appeared yet. My eldest grandson always speaks of my "joimping up and down" on winter Sundays to keep the buckwheat cakes flowing from stove to table, and true it is that to be served in bulk and peace, pancakes should have an assistant in the kitchen. Looking forward to that happy day, let's have a recipe or two. These should feed four but the amounts are not guaranteed against appetites.

For real old-fashioned BUCKWHEAT CAKES put 1 cup of warm water in a wide-mouthed 2 or 3-quart pitcher. Add 1 teaspoon of sugar, 2 tablespoons of white or yellow cornmeal, 1 tablespoon of white flour, and ½ teaspoon of salt. Beat in 2 or 2½ cups of buckwheat flour to make a thick batter. Dissolve ¼ of a yeast cake in ½ cup of lukewarm water, add to the batter, give it one final beating, cover the pitcher, and let stand overnight in a warm place. Next morning dissolve 1 tablespoon of New Orleans molasses and ½ teaspoon of baking soda in ¾ cup of boiling water. Beat it in and add a little more water if necessary to make a thin batter. Grease your hot griddle with a bit of salt pork rind or bacon and bake the cakes. This was my grandmother's recipe and like all old ones was originally even vaguer as to proportions than as given here. Even now it is impossible to allow for the variations in flour, but one try will convince you how simple, easy and cheap, too, the cakes are to make.

My SOUR MILK HOT CAKES are almost as delicate as French crêpes. Separate 2 eggs, beat the whites stiff, and continue with the same beater on the yolks until they are thick. Sift 1½ cups of flour with 1 tablespoon of white or yellow cornmeal, 1 tablespoon of sugar, ½ teaspoon of salt, ½ teaspoon of baking soda, and ½ teaspoon of baking powder. Add alternately to the yolks with 2 cups of sour thick milk. (If necessary measure this out 24 hours ahead and let it get well curdled in a warm place, or use buttermilk instead.) Gently fold in the beaten egg whites and stir in 2 tablespoons of cooking oil, and bake on a hot, lightly greased griddle, turning only once.

SOUR MILK WAFFLES have a flavor that no bought mix has ever achieved. Beat the whites of 3 eggs stiff, then tackle their yolks. Sift 2 cups of flour twice with 1 teaspoon of baking soda, ½ teaspoon of salt, and 3 teaspoons of sugar. Add alternately to the yolks with 2 cups of sour milk or buttermilk. Fold in the egg whites and 5 tablespoons of cooking oil. The waffle iron should need no greasing.

When once impressed with the ease with which company for breakfast can be handled, don't be surprised to find yourself issuing invitations for a large buffet affair on Sunday morning. This is even more fun when planned to follow a special occasion like a wedding, dance or someone else's (not your) large party the day before, for from boarding school days on humanity seems to love to get together the next morning for a thorough rehash of the last night's happenings. A menu of kidney stew, scrambled eggs, waffles and coffee automatically suggests itself as delicious and capable of being prepared ahead. Set the table and have the stew made the night before, and even the waffle batter can be mixed without soda and baking powder and covered in the icebox ready for the addition of the leavening before cooking. If you use a mix for this have the eggs and milk that it calls for already measured. Then tuck yourself in for a peaceful night's sleep. Next morning make the eggs at the table over an electric stove or that almost forgotten but still useful adjunct of the 1900s, a chafing dish. Give the waffle iron into the care of one of the culinary experts who always yearn to assist the hostess, bring in pitchers of iced tomato juice, plenty of hot coffee, and the party is on!

My friend Mrs. Yellott is famed far beyond her native Baltimore for her magnificent Maryland Hunt Cup breakfasts held the morning after that great horse race. The throng of guests can choose between the delights of fried tomatoes, kidney stew, eggs and bacon, broiled sweetbreads, and even homemade sausage with waffles, besides their fruit juice and coffee, and her menu is a bit overwhelming for any but a born cook with capable aid. But her welcoming snifter of Champagne is worth copying at a simpler breakfast party and with good domestic wine needn't add much to the expense. Try the whole menu sometime for a special occasion when you want to splurge, and have the green and gold bottles in an ice-filled bucket, ready to greet nightworn eyes.

The younger fry, debutante age and up (heaven forbid that I should trespass in those forgotten, horror-filled lands of real "children's parties"), love a breakfast, too. The food needn't be so elaborate, but lots of waffles, from two irons if possible, two or three sweet spreads, creamed dried beef, and not so much coffee as their elders—they don't need it, bless 'em—will produce screams of delight, especially if each one is given a heavy china "dog wagon" coffee mug, painted with their respective names, initials, or some personal joke. Use a quick drying enamel for the art work. Add a Victrola with some new jazz records and you have a shindig that will last well into the afternoon. And if then you roll in a small keg of iced beer and produce the same cups (washed) for that, while passing wooden bowls of pretzels and popcorn, well, you're a member of the gang for life! And don't say I didn't warn you!

Less Moaning
at the Bar, Please

My father adored city life. "Lowing cattle!" he'd say, "Give me clanging trolleys," and only a strong sense of family duty forced him to the purchase of a suburban home when I was about eight. There, for six years, he unhappily shoveled snow, ran for trains, and evaded Mother's attempts to interest him in gardening, consoled by the thought that his children were being raised in health-giving "country air."

The public school was too far away for my younger brother and sister, the nearby private school very expensive, so to the satisfaction of Mother's yearning for British upper-class life and Father's Quaker thrift, three miserable little Americans were taught all one long winter by an English governess.

Poor Miss Follansbee! A pathetic expatriated worshipper of Alfred, Lord Tennyson, we held her completely responsible for the loss of our sociable school life, and her mild, "My dears, not so much vulgarity" was a feeble restraint on young hooligans long inured to a frequently applied parental hairbrush. Spring saw her welcome departure for, I hope, a happier situation, leaving us with temporary Oxford accents, a fine contempt for all things English, and a permanent loathing of her favorite poem "Crossing the Bar." "Sunset and evening star…" Piffle! Turned loose every summer in small boats, we knew able seamen had no time to waste on scenery when over dangerous shoals, and we scorned the Victorian tearjerker as well as its landlubber author. But with age has come a belated appreciation of the Dear Queen's beloved Poet Laureate, even though neither he nor his ruler would approve of my modern interpretation of the lyrics. Nevertheless far too much moaning still goes on when the average female is confronted with the task of mixing and serving drinks.

There is no gainsaying the accepted male responsibility for the liquid refreshments, but when the hostess lives alone and likes it or the host is delayed beyond the arrival of the guests, any halfway intelligent woman should be able to produce a drinkable cocktail, for no matter how men delight in making the mixing mysterious, a dry martini, for instance, takes even less time and much less skill than baking a plain cake, and no loss of femininity ever follows the discovery that the contents of the cook's frosty shaker are palatable. Rather, there comes the assurance that the meal to follow will be even more delicious than expected, and an added charm to her already becoming apron.

If it is necessary to start from scratch and attend to the purchasing as well as to the mixing, remember that no male ever failed the appeal of a helpless (*sic*) woman, and ask the advice of the liquor-store salesman as to the best brands.

Eschew fancy glasses and shakers. Plain, clear crystal, expensive or cheap, allows the contents to meet the eye of its consumer boldly and untroubled by garish tints or ungrippable tortured stems. When a wealthy friend proudly displayed her latest set of imported glassware—"reasonable facsimiles" of the Goddess of Liberty bearing a colored bowl on her head— my only reaction was not envy but a slight nausea which was only cured by going home to gaze with renewed affection at my own three-for-a-quarter window-pane tumblers. Another advantage of plain glass is its easy replacement. Great-grandmother's dinner china may descend complete to generation after generation but it's rare when a dozen highball glasses remain intact through as many months. Put your money in unobtrusive patterns or into "open stock" that can be filled without showing too glaring a difference.

Measure ingredients carefully with a regulation jigger, have plenty of ice, for much good liquor has been ruined by inadequate chilling, and finally go easy on the garnishing of the drinks. Dashing members of the Tuesday luncheon and bridge club may relish a sweet weak cocktail with trimmings that resemble low tide at Coney Island but a true *bon vivant* prefers the bouquet of his liquor unspoiled.

Attention, female bartenders! Let's go. The first lesson is a recipe for the drink that, according to Dr. Gallup and his fellow snoopers, is the most popular, a simple DRY MARTINI. 3 parts gin and 1 part French vermouth, poured over egg-sized pieces of ice in a pitcher. Stir lightly until cold but do not shake, for too vigorous treatment is supposed to "bruise" the mixture. Strain and serve in glasses with a green olive in the bottom of each and a twist of lemon peel on top. Make only enough at one time for a single round. Small pickled onions may replace the olives, without the drink losing social standing, although the same can't be said of the drinkers, and a handful of fresh mint leaves in the mixing pitcher is approved by many.

A PERFECT COCKTAIL is a dry martini with half the French vermouth replaced by an equal quantity of the Italian variety, and is a little sweeter as a result.

MANHATTAN. 3 parts rye whisky to 1 part Italian vermouth. Shake well in an iced container and serve with a maraschino cherry in each glass. Bartenders are no more subtle than cooks, so by now you should easily be expert enough to guess that a DRY MANHATTAN uses French vermouth in the same proportion.

An OLD-FASHIONED COCKTAIL should be leisurely in both the mixing and imbibing. Using good-sized tumblers with thick bottoms—eight ounces aren't a bit too large—put 1 teaspoon of sugar or half a lump in each. Add 1 tablespoon of water and muddle or crush the sugar. Add 1 dash of Angostura bitters and 1 jigger of rye whisky. Put in 2 or 3 chunks of ice, twist a bit of lemon peel over the top, and give a glass to each guest with a small muddler or spoon, to stir and sip at his ease. These are best not attempted in bulk. One dear old soul I know sought to cheer the local "Ladies Aid" on a chilly day by mixing old-fashioneds and serving them from a teapot. Some of the members are still a little hazy as to what went on at the meeting afterwards. Old-fashioneds can be made with Scotch whisky, when they become ROB ROYS, or with bourbon and a few leaves of mint crushed with the sugar. These last are called BABY'S MINT JULEP, though heaven help the infant that downs one.

RUM OLD-FASHIONEDS demand light rum in place of whisky, can be garnished with lime instead of lemon, and are otherwise made just as in the preceding recipe. A most refreshing drink for a hot evening, we first learned of them on a trip to those lovely and little-known West Indian islands that dot the Caribbean Sea below Cuba like the beads of a broken necklace. Rhum Martinique was their foundation then, and the harassed bar steward of our crowded British freighter considered us real "quality" because we ordered them only before dinner and stuck to a bottle of Guinness with lunch.

STRAWBERRY BLOSSOM. Press the juice from 1 quart of ripe strawberries. Strain and add 1 tablespoon of lemon juice to each cupful. Sweeten slightly, the amount of sugar varying with the tartness of the berries. Add 1 jigger of gin and 1 tablespoon of heavy cream to each jigger of juice, shake well with plenty of ice, and serve in martini glasses. This is a perfect porch drink for the more daring "girls" and so is the following mild DAIQUIRI: Dissolve 1 teaspoon of powdered sugar in the juice of 1 lime. Add 1 jigger of

Bacardi rum, stir, and pour slowly into a Champagne or fruit compote glass that has first been packed with finely crushed ice. Decorate with a strawberry or cherry and sip through a short straw.

SHERRY or GIN "AND" are English aperitifs much superior to most of that island's cooking. Put a good dash of Angostura bitters in a sherry glass and roll it around until the inside is thoroughly coated. Drain out any drops that remain and fill the glass with gin or dry sherry. A twist of lemon peel is an optional garnish and, with the recipes coming from overseas, there naturally need be no chilling of either drink.

For that dreaded but often necessary large party, with no assistant bartender, a drink that can be made well ahead of time is usually easier to serve than cocktails. FISH HOUSE PUNCH, known and appreciated by George Washington, is without a peer in this category, but should be served with caution to the uninitiated. Looking and tasting almost as mild as Coca-Cola, it has scored more knockouts than Joe Louis himself. So keep a watchful eye on any rich unsophisticated maiden aunt's trips to the source of supply, for while with her second cup she may well begin writing checks in your favor for astronomical amounts, after the third or fourth beaker her illegible signature is likely to leave the way open for later unjustified charges of forgery. Facing possible results cheerfully, proceed with the mixing. Thoroughly dissolve ¾ pound of sugar (lump if possible) in just enough water to take up the sugar. Add 1 quart of fresh strained lemon juice, 2 quarts Jamaica rum, 1 quart cognac, 2 quarts water, and ½ cup peach brandy. Allow this to brew 2 or 3 hours or overnight, in a corked demijohn in a cool spot, then an hour or two before serving pour it into a punch bowl over a big piece of ice.

CHAMPAGNE PUNCH is milder, perhaps safer, and much simpler to make. Add ½ cup brandy to 1 quart champagne, add an optional bottle of sauterne, and serve poured over a hard-frozen block of orange water ice. This is refreshing and, made with a good domestic Champagne needn't be too expensive.

My father always said that SAUTERNE or RHINE WINE CUP had no equal as a cooler on a hot summer day. He "imported" the wine by the barrel inexpensively from California and a particularly hideous cut glass pitcher was kept sacred to its mixing. I was sometimes allowed a small sip after the ice had become well melted, and was almost grown-up before I realized that white wine didn't carry a delicate scent of cucumber. When I married and made—to him—an incomprehensible move to the suburbs, he always saw that we too had a plentiful hot weather supply of his favorite vintage, and I learned to have the cup ready and waiting whenever he took the "exhausting" 15 minute journey to discover how things were progressing out in the sticks. Its mixing requires very little effort and few ingredients. Put 1 teaspoon of sugar into a tall pitcher, dissolve it with a little water, then put in 2 or 3 good-sized pieces of ice. Carefully insert 2 long slices of well-washed cucumber rind between the ice and the glass to lend their cool green glow to the drink. Pour in 1 bottle of Rhine wine or dry sauterne and 1 pint, or a little more, of sparkling water, give it a stir, and "drink till cold." This can be braced a bit with a jigger of brandy and a few slices of orange or lemon, although the original is hard to improve upon. To those uneducated souls who complain of the cucumber flavor, simply murmur with raised eyebrows that the emerald garnish gives the drink the exact taste of borage, an herb that since Charlemagne's day has been considered the perfect partner of white wine.

For years, one of the city's leading physicians was our near neighbor. So beloved he was by his patients that when he entered politics it was rumored that many about-to-be-mothers planned their infants' arrivals with Election Day and a vote for their adored doctor in mind. His busy life left little room for entertaining. Only his New Year's afternoon remained sacred, and below is the recipe for the famous EGGNOG he and his pretty wife dispensed then to numerous friends. Beat the yolks of 6 eggs thoroughly with ¾ cup of sugar. Slowly stir in 2 quarts of rich milk and, just as slowly, 1 pint of rye whisky and 1 tablespoon of rum. Fold in the stiffly beaten whites of 6 eggs and chill overnight if you wish. Dust with nutmeg before serving.

The paint on the "Bar and Grill" that appeared surprisingly at a dusty crossroads was so new that we were almost afraid the spotless building was a mirage caused by famished heat-dazed eyes, for we had spent a long antiquarian morning searching the New Jersey barrens for the vanished foundations of a pre-Revolutionary iron furnace. While I attended to the ordering of our meal in a cedar-lined dining room, my husband disappeared into the bar and returned with two frosted glasses of draught ale. Placing them on our red-checked tablecloth, he put his head in his hands in such a silent fit of choking hysterics that I was sure the midday sun had done its worst. For minutes the only intelligible reply to my frenzied questions was "The sign! The sign!" Finally obeying his pleading gestures I tiptoed to the door of the crowded little bar and was immediately overcome with my own attack of repressed laughter. On the shining bar mirror, embellished with the flourishes beloved by bartenders since the world began, I too, had seen the words "Try our GUADALCANAL PIGEONS MILK. It restores Vitality and increases Productiveness." The knowledge of this potion seemed a much more important addition to our country's history than the once desired furnace site. Here is how the newly returned veteran host mixed it: Put ½ jigger of brandy, ½ jigger of rum, and 1 cup of rich milk into a shaker. Add 1 raw egg, 1 teaspoon of sugar, and 2 or 3 big pieces of ice. Shake until frothy, then strain into a highball glass. Since its discovery we have delighted many people with this, and while its qualities don't entirely live up to the original advertisement, its quaffing is nevertheless nourishing and refreshing.

Of all our failings, our dislike of BARLEY WATER rankled most in Miss Follansbee's heart. Here is how she drank it, for them that wants to follow her example. Wash 1 teaspoon of pearl barley, add to it 2 cups of boiling water, and cook 2 hours in a covered double boiler. Strain and add the juice of ½ lemon, a few slivers of the fruit, and 1 tablespoon or more of sugar.

Chill, but leave out ice, and serve when stumps are drawn after the cricket match.

Good American LEMONADE is much more thirst quenching. Boil ¾ cup of sugar with 2 cups of water until dissolved. Cool slightly and add ½ cup or more of strained lemon juice. This foundation syrup can be kept covered in the refrigerator for 2 or 3 days. When ready to drink, dilute it to taste, with water and serve it in ice-filled glasses. Made in larger quantities, garnished with mint, strawberries and pineapple, this makes a very good temperance punch.

HORSE'S NECK. Remove the peel from a lemon in one long spiral and line a tall glass with it. Add 2 or 3 chunks of ice and fill up the glass with ginger ale. This will be appreciated by the most ardent non-teetotaler after a hard set of tennis.

OLD-FASHIONED RASPBERRY VINEGAR, with its tart flavor, is a summer refresher that shouldn't be forgotten. Cover 2 quarts of ripe crushed

raspberries with 1 quart of good cider vinegar. Keep covered in a bowl or crock for 2 days, then drain and repeat with 2 fresh quarts of berries. Drain again, this time through a cloth. To every pint of juice allow a pound of sugar. Boil until the sugar is dissolved—about 5 minutes—then skim, and if it is not to be used immediately, bottle and seal as in the recipe for tomato catsup on page 129. To serve, put a jigger of the vinegar into a tall glass, add a few pieces of ice, and fill up the glass with carbonated water. This is much like the French "sirop" that boulevardiers enjoy. I loved it as a child and still do, but my own children preferred HOMEMADE ICE-CREAM SODAS. Put ½ cup of cold rich milk in a tall glass, add a good dollop of any preferred ice cream, and fill with carbonated water. Stir thoroughly to raise a professional-looking "head" on the soda, and serve with a straw and a long spoon. A fine light lunch with a few salty crackers on the side.

All drinks, be they nonalcoholic or the opposite, should be served in ample but not overwhelming quantities. Many a young tummy has suffered just as much from an excess of lemonade as one older and equally less wise from too frequent rounds of martinis. Better, of course, that the hostess be generous than stingy, still a happy medium should be firmly adhered to, for though King Solomon sang "Stay me with flagons" to the Queen of Sheba, she knew when to stop both the flagons and the staying, and history never mentions his hanging around her tent with his attendants, caroling the Old Testament equivalent of "Sweet Adeline" until the neighboring tribes complained.

Hors-d'œuvres served in bulk have as deleterious an effect on a guest's digestion as overindulgence in the cocktails they accompany and, in addition, are apt to deaden all interest in the meal to follow, a calamity no cook cares to contemplate. Something should be done about this menace to dinner-table enjoyment, and like all good Americans when faced with a problem, my first instinct is to form a "committee."

An easily amused group, we have had numerous family clubs, some of short duration like the "Be-Kind-to-Daddy Association," disbanded after its beneficiary and self-elected president of the "Eight Ball Society" found its purpose boring. "Ghouls Union, Local No. 1" seemed doomed, too, when its members, my daughter and I, mistakenly called her father's attention to the prize find of an old New England tombstone which had his initials carved over an affecting epitaph, but it was revived during subsequent motor trips and we continue a happy correspondence on the Union's discoveries in ancient graveyards.

The new club I am about to found deserves a larger permanent membership, all pledged to the dual objectives of limiting cocktail parties to a dozen well-selected guests and the serving thereat of not more than two kinds of appetizers. High time it is to curtail the big boring gatherings with their warm, badly-mixed drinks, and especially the trays of assorted foods that resemble a Sunday School picnic. Appetizers should be just what their name implies, *not* a full course meal, and a small selection with well-iced dry cocktails are all that any dinner needs for a perfect start.

Club members will be allowed an ice-filled bowl of ripe and green olives that have been drained after an overnight soaking in garlic-flavored French dressing, or canned button mushrooms treated the same way for a delicious change, and let the accompanying platter hold one of the following:

CHEESE PÂTÉ NUMBER 1. This recipe was bribed years ago from the chef of a famous hotel where a high-priced slice still leads the list of hors-d'œuvres. Use a round-bottomed bowl and with a silver fork crumble and cream ¼ pound of well-aged Roquefort cheese until not a lump remains. Mix in 2 tablespoons of finely minced chives or ½ teaspoon of scraped onion. Add 2 small packages, or ¼ pound, of cream cheese, and blend well before thinning with ½ cup of dry sherry. Add ½ teaspoon of salt, ¼ teaspoon of hand-ground black pepper, a few grains of cayenne, and 1 tablespoon of Hungarian paprika. Replace the last item with the domestic if necessary. Mix all thoroughly, form the pâté into a roll, wrap it in wax paper, and let it season and harden overnight in the refrigerator.

CHEESE PÂTÉ NUMBER 2. Mix the same amount of cream cheese as above with 1 tablespoon of anchovy paste. This can be served immediately, as can CHEESE PÂTÉ NUMBER 3, in which the cream cheese is mixed with ½ cup of minced chives and seasoned with salt and black pepper.

SHRIMP PÂTÉ. Remove the black veins from 2 cups of canned or cooked shelled shrimps and put them twice through the fine cutter of the food chopper. Melt ¼ cup of butter with 1 bruised clove of garlic. Remove the garlic and add the butter to the shrimps. Stir in ¼ cup of tart mayonnaise, ½ teaspoon of salt, ¼ teaspoon of black pepper, and perhaps a few drops of Worcestershire sauce and tomato catsup. Form into a roll, wrap and chill as in Cheese Pâté, Number 1.

AVOCADO PÂTÉ. Using a silver fork again, make a paste of 1 ripe peeled avocado pear. Add ½ cup of minced watercress, 2 tablespoons of French dressing, 1 teaspoon of Worcestershire sauce, and a scrape of onion. Add ¼ teaspoon each of salt and black pepper and a good dash of cayenne, as this must be really hot. It is a Puerto Rican recipe and down there they like to overcome the bland flavor of the avocado. You might serve this heaped high in half of the avocado shell.

All of these pâtés are better if, instead of being spread beforehand, they are brought in cold in a bowl or small casserole, surrounded with toast, salt crackers or thin quarter-slices of rye bread, so that your guests may help themselves.

MUSHROOM CANAPÉS. Chop finely, or grind, ½ pound of washed un-peeled whole mushrooms. Melt 2 tablespoons of butter, blend in 1 table-spoon of flour, and add the mushrooms and 2 tablespoons of cream. Season with salt and black pepper. Cool and spread on individual rounds of toast.

CUCUMBER CANAPÉS. Toast the necessary number of bread rounds. Mix mayonnaise with ½ its quantity of chopped watercress and spread thinly on each circle. Top with a thin slice of unpeeled cucumber, that has been marinated in French dressing. Decorate with a slice of red radish.

SHRIMPS WITH CURRIED MAYONNAISE. Just that! Put rows of cooked peeled or canned shrimps on a platter and place in the center a bowl filled with 1 cup of mayonnaise (page 102) mixed with 1 teaspoon of curry powder. Raw CAULIFLOWER flowerets that have been first crisped in ice water are delicious and different served this way, too.

CHEESE WHIRLS can be made ahead. Use half the recipe for piecrust (page 117), divide the crust, and roll each half into a thin rectangle about 4 inches wide and cover each thickly with 1 cup of finely grated sharp American cheese. Add salt and a dash of cayenne. Roll up loosely and dampen the far edge of the crust with icewater and seal firmly. Chill. Cut each roll into ½-inch slices with a sharp knife, flick each with paprika, place on a greased cooky sheet, and bake 5 minutes in a 400° oven.

HAM PUFFS mustn't be kept waiting. Mix ½ teaspoon of dry mustard with a 4 ounce can of deviled ham. Add ½ cup of finely grated Parmesan cheese and a few grains of cayenne. Fold into the stiffly beaten white of 1 egg. Toast 12 or 15 small rounds of bread on one side. Heap the teaspoonfuls of ham mixture on the toasted side, place on a cooky sheet, and bake 5 minutes in a 450° oven.

Thin crosscuts of CANNED FRANKFURTERS on TOOTHPICKS, topped with a small pickled onion, are good quickly made appetizers, and so are POTATO CHIPS dusted with grated Parmesan cheese and a little cayenne and then heated in a 400° oven for 5 minutes.

Thin slices of bought LUNCHEON MEAT or BOLOGNA made into sandwiches filled with seasoned cream cheese and cut into thin wedges take very little time.

With the savings from their economical selection of appetizers club members will be able to afford more frequently the finest taste-teaser of all: CAVIAR, black or red. It too goes in a bowl, over chopped ice and tastes best resting on slivers of dark pumpernickel. A bylaw allows us to have on special occasions such as birthdays a CANAPÉ CAKE with its three distinct fillings. Remove the crusts and cut four thin slices from the center of a round loaf of rye or white bread. Butter the bottom piece lightly and spread with ½ cup of Cheese Pâté Number 1 (above). Cover with a second buttered slice and spread that with ½ cup of deviled ham mixed with 1 tablespoon of mayonnaise and a little hot mustard. Put on the third layer and butter. On that can go ½ cup of chopped cucumbers thinned with a little mayonnaise, or ½ cup of Shrimp Pâté (above). Clap on the fourth slice and ice the whole thing with 2 packages of cream cheese diluted with ½ cup of cream or top milk. Decorate the icing with curlicues of anchovy paste forced from the tube and tiny red cocktail onions for color. Place in a cool spot for 2 or 3 hours and let the guest of honor cut the first thin slice.

As Alexander Woollcott used to say, "Won't you join my frat?"

Hot Stuff for the Range Owner

Like the forever unsettled, "Which came first, the chicken or the egg?", that other question "which is more necessary in the house, the bed or the stove?" has almost as much chance of being satisfactorily answered. Granted that the three most important happenings in life, birth, marriage and death, take place in bed; three equally vital occurrences, breakfast, lunch and dinner, daily owe their success to the stove.

There are substitutes for many household furnishings. Orange crates may pinch-hit for chairs, a barrel doesn't make a bad table, and conscienceless borrowing, as we all know to our sorrow, has too often produced an impressive library, but there is no substitute for either good food or a comfortable bed. A meal cooked with difficulty is a sorry prelude to an undisturbed night's sleep and vice-versa, as the Tweedles Dum and Dee used to say to each other. Perhaps the safest advice to budding householders with a thin pocketbook is to halve their budget, buy the best bed and stove they can afford, and raid the family attics for the balance of their furnishings. Don't rush either purchase, for these important articles, like a husband, should last a lifetime if well selected.

Except under the heading of "entertainment," advice on beds isn't appropriate in a cookbook, but here goes on stoves, from a long and varied experience that begins with the wood-alcohol holocaust of my early youth, through later struggles in the galley of a small boat with a two-hole woodburning "Shipmate," up to my present kitchen marvel that does everything but wag its tail on order.

Electric stoves are perhaps more modern and definitely cleaner than gas. They take a little longer to arrive at the desired heat, but once properly set the heat remains constant and a meal can be left cooking for any length of time, safe in the knowledge that nothing will boil over or burn. Nor will you be met at the kitchen door by a gust of asphyxiating air. For this last reason, I feel they are a "must," if possible, in the house with small children. On the other hand, those who swear by a gas stove (and they are legion) stoutly maintain that their method of cooking is quicker and, in most localities, cheaper, too. A good combination is a gas stove and a large electric table oven for big slow pot roasts, or the extra pie or cake that there isn't room for in an already full stove oven. Do try to have two ovens. One seems all that is necessary to a beginner but as you become more proficient you'll often want to get a lot of baking over with at one time. Never will I forget the wonder on a young bride's face when I complained that my present oven "only held four loaves of bread," but within a year she was on the phone to inquire where a spare could be purchased.

A separate broiler or "barbecuer" is a most useful addition to any stove, but I've never been able to see the advantages of the so-called "deep-well thrift cooker." Since I think that any cooking can be done just as economically on a regulation top-burner, I had my thrift job replaced by one burner, and now enjoy space for an extra pan of my own choice.

With the stove once decided upon, the next question is, of course, its location in the kitchen, and this, too, should be given long deep thought. The dealer from whom you purchase it will probably be of help, but stand out for a good working light, plenty of room in front and at the sides, the correct height for you, and a shelf over it for seasonings. This last should be fairly narrow, but longer than you think necessary at first, for as time goes on more and more small bottles and boxes will find a home there. Mine at this moment supports not only the conventional salt, pepper and flour, but shakers of mustard, sugar, chili and curry powder, 4 or 5 different spices and herbs, bottles of meat sauces, and two cruets of cooking wine, for nothing so aggravates my impatient soul as to have to hunt for the desired flavoring just as a dish is nearly at perfection. A hook for pot-holders is a help, and some cooks like to keep their most-used small pots and pans hanging near.

Even with your stove installed you're not through with it and I give you this last most important advice. *Get acquainted with it* before you look for its best performances. No one expects a newly bought puppy, no matter how beguiling, to be housebroken or to perform tricks, and very few people, thank Heaven, get unduly intimate when first introduced. Don't think that the spotless new stove will show all its good—or bad—qualities the minute you meet. Like a friend-to-be, you'll have to cultivate the good and ignore or kindly pass over its unpleasant traits. My present kitchen-confidante has unsatisfactory overhead light and the ingenuity of a graduate of M.I.T. is required to remove the drip pan, while I would no more think of gossiping about the bottom drawer's habit of spilling out skillets than I would of criticizing a good friend's new hairdo.

Pots and pans come next in your kitchen furniture. Go slow with your purchases here, too, and keep to the family motto that "only the best is good enough," for utensils, like the stove, should last a long while. If you must economize, start with a few expensive ones, fill in from the five-and-dime, and then replace the cheaper articles as they wear—and wear out they will, never fear—with better quality.

The foundation of an efficient *batterie de cuisine* is a large, heavy cast-iron skillet or frying pan with a tight-fitting lid. Unless it comes with more explicit directions from the manufacturer, before you use them scrub the pan and its lid well with steel wool, then dry them and coat the inside of each thoroughly with unsalted grease. Lard or cooking oil will do. Put them in a warm oven or over a low burner for 2 or 3 hours and at intervals swab on more grease, if the first has been absorbed. Like a dry skin, new iron takes to lubrication. Let them cool, wipe off any remaining grease with a paper towel, and they are ready to serve you. Again like a dry skin, water should touch the iron from now on as rarely as possible, so after frying bacon or potatoes in it, simply pour out the remaining grease and use the paper towel once more. With this tender treatment it will last for years, smooth and unrusted. I still possess the original I started housekeeping with many years ago, but have lost count of the cheaper thin ones I've discarded. While the lovely gleaming aluminum fryers are fine for chicken or deep-fat cooking, when it comes to sautéing or pan-broiling meat, or for hashed brown potatoes, nothing takes the place of an old black pal. It can be used to boil, stew or roast too, and a big fellow will do well by a small amount of food, but no vice versa in this case.

The next purchase should be a set of deep saucepans, also with tight lids. Aluminum comes into its own for these, as does the lovely and expensive stainless steel. They generally come two or three in a cozy nest, can be used for mixing bowls or a double boiler, and with them, your big skillet, and the coffee pot of your choice you can take your time about the rest of your equipment.

A paring knife is indicated here—possibly two—one with a short fat blade and the other with a long thin cutting edge. Many cooks claim that a good parer should cost at least seventy-five cents but if you cultivate a friendly butcher when it comes to the cutlery department, you'll get better steel and a cheaper article. I successfully wheedled three allegedly worn-out small knives—at a small price, too—out of my meat provider and their efficient shape and keenness make them a constant joy. Add a couple of wooden spoons with their handles cut off halfway down for easy grasping, and you're ready for fancy cooking, although an old-fashioned cook would be shocked at the absence of the tea kettle that once adorned every coal range. But what's a saucepan for if not to boil water? After becoming used to a few kitchen utensils, you'll know what other things you really need. Now consider a roaster, a few mixing bowls, earthenware casseroles, and pans for cake and pie. These last can be of glass, and if space as well as expense is a consideration, one shape can be used for both. Get your iron skillet collection started soon, too. I've finally ended up with four, the big one I began with, two of medium size, one of which I try to keep for fish, and a much smaller one that fries or scrambles one or two eggs, or browns a few onions for flavoring sauces or gravy.

Having a family known for their casual approach to the hours for meals, double boilers come next to skillets in my affection, and like the famous nursery bears, three of these food-warmers seem just an adequate number. The big daddy holds almost a gallon and comes out only for parties, when it is invaluable for keeping food at the right temperature; a middle-sized momma is used for the morning oatmeal and for making a custard or any dish to which eggs or cheese are to be added; and a baby, holding a pint, melts butter or chocolate, makes hollandaise or béarnaise sauce or fluffy icing, heats up leftover vegetables, and is, as a matter of fact, more useful than the other two together, although mine is the only kitchen in which I've seen its like. This is one of my favorite utensils and woe betide the helper who uses the top compartment as a "singleton."

Sets of tin canisters and their big matching boxes for bread and cake are leftovers from Grandmother's kitchen that we can well do without. Coffee and tea both arrive nowadays in their own airtight containers, while the refrigerator or freezer is the place for that extra loaf of bread. Cake takes to a cool place, too. Try to find a small tin or steel "dispatch" box that will hold the loaf in use and there will be just so much less clutter on your shelves. A heavy piece of cotton duck instead of a breadboard is another space-saver, and if you can have an old marble bureau top set in your work table that's even better for rolling out piecrust or dough.

The only redeeming feature of the pipe my husband is never without and its consequent litter of ashes, cleaners and burnt matches is the lovely wide-mouthed glass jars in which his tobacco comes. These are just right for dry groceries like beans and lentils, barley, rice, other cereals, or crackers. Wash them and their tops with hot soap suds, give them a scalding bath, fit a fresh piece of waxed cardboard or paper into the lids, and behold cheap, airtight, sanitary, and easily stacked containers where you can see at a glance just when the contents need replenishing. Paint the tops and decorate them with cutouts or decalcomanias for real style. If your man isn't a pipe addict, try wangling a few big empty candy jars out of the proprietor of the corner store. What you want is something large enough to get a hand or small measuring cup into.

Once settled with a stove and started off on a collection of adequate utensils, the sink is the next big problem. And again, don't forget the family motto and the fact that it, too, needs plenty of light and room and must be installed at the correct height. The cost of a few extra inches of pipe will more than repay you for the backaches you won't get. A mixing spigot and drain boards on both sides are helps towards really streamlined dishwashing, although mechanical marvels in that line are promised. Until these prove their worth, hie yourself to a good hotel supply store for a big wire dish drainer—one about half again as wide, high and long as the usual home variety. With its aid, and a plentiful supply of hot water, plates and pans for twenty people will be out of the way in as many minutes.

While on the subject of modern improvements watch with a leery eye the great stretches of linoleum work surfaces that architects are so busy install-ing in our kitchens. They are a sticky resting place for hot pans, and while the linoleum can be scraped or burnt off a favorite skillet or casserole, the lovely work surface suffers permanently. Hold out for a few useful stretches of old-fashioned hardwood near your serving table or stove. Linoleum on the floor, however, is a never-ending delight. Let it run from wall to wall if possible and pick your design not only for color but, even more important, for its nondirt-showing qualities. A beautiful clear pattern is likely to lose its appeal quickly when it calls for constant scrubbing.

The cook, who uses them most, should be allowed the final decision concerning the sink, stove, and its utensils, but the habits of the whole family should be taken into consideration when it comes to the last important purchase for the kitchen—the refrigerator. Too often only the electric type is considered, forgetting that while it heralds the welcome disappearance of the iceman, that bringer-in of mud and gossip and sex interest, there also often vanishes a really adequate, bountiful supply of ice. Millionaires, of course, have none of this problem but, for a large less-prosperous family with a passion for homemade ice cream and frequent guests, a big modern icebox is really much more practical than the smaller, equally priced electric refrigerator. For years I kept food cold and fresh in a large top-icer, constantly amused at the friends who laughed at my old-fashioned ideas but never hesitated to put in frantic calls for room to take care of an especially large roast or the "lend" of a piece of ice. When our family became smaller we stored the big box, being able to afford what was for the two of us an adequate electric refrigerator, and I would be the last to deny the superior comfort and delight it provides. But when the children began reappearing with wives, husbands and grandchildren, the old faithful friend was reinstated and it welcomed thrice weekly with open doors and roomy shelves not only twenty bottles of milk but the beer, Coca-Cola and ginger ale that our much increased group again demanded. Like an electric or gas stove, the two kinds of coolers both have their points and if you can't swing financially the big electric refrigerator you know is necessary, either get a really good large modern icebox or buy the smaller electric article and find room in the cellar or on the back porch for an assistant, ready to be filled with ice and to take care of extras and leftovers.

All of this advice is just for the foundation of a culinary tool shop, and doesn't even touch the department where most of us are complete pushovers and, as in other sadder matters, "stoop to folly and find too late that men betray." Those intriguing kitchen gadgets! While glamour girls linger before Hattie Carnegie's latest display, and men have to be dragged from a shop filled with sporting goods, any real woman will take a good country fair, there to watch entranced the slick demonstration of the latest can opener or apple corer. My kitchen walls look like an old-fashioned tin peddler's cart. The shamefaced admission that a great many tricky articles have been thrown away almost as soon as bought eases the conscience. However, a surprising number of the devices purchased while under the hypnotic influence of a sideshow barker have turned out to be both useful and labor saving. What looks like a midget posthole digger removes the hard center from grapefruit with a minimum of effort. The "swivel" potato peeler takes off a thin rind that even the most Scotch housewife would approve, and the grater that I bore home so proudly from the Atlantic City Boardwalk shreds carrots or slices cucumbers paper thin with equal ease. But heed two warnings, kitchen gadgeteers! First follow the manufacturer's directions when you try out your new treasure, and second, find it a resting place where it will be at hand when wanted. Even that super-gadget, an electric mixer, should stand ready to be put to work at the small jobs it does just as well as the big ones, and I ask, "What good is a wall can opener—and every kitchen should have one—if it remains in a drawer waiting for the never-present handyman to put it up?"

Now let's get on to the only kind of interior decorating—besides food—that belongs in this volume, and have a few recipes whose ingredients are the four walls that are about to hem in you and your stove. Poor Mrs. Rorer and her generation were committed to depressing bilious yellow or equally dirt-resisting chocolate-colored surroundings. Then came the other extreme, a passion for asepsis, with cold, white enamel and sanitary, snowy, uninspiring tile.

Kitchens nowadays have other standards. Besides efficiency, they should express their owner's personality and be a happy spot in which to work. Men display their tastes and hobbies in their offices and why shouldn't women do the same in their kitchens? So, if you're a blond with an unsatisfied longing for pale pink and blue, go ahead, paint your "office" walls in one of those colors, the woodwork in the other, hang up sheer feminine curtains, and discover how much more pleasant even dull potato peeling is in a becoming environment.

One of the most charming kitchens I know, ruled over by a luscious brunette, has lipstick red trim and wide ruffled curtains of unbleached muslin billowing at the sunny windows, while the cream-colored unfinished plaster walls are marked off in half-yard squares where friends have written and autographed their favorite recipes. Effective, original and cheap! Another dark-haired chef basks against a chartreuse background, deep burgundy woodwork, and touches of bright royal blue. Around the walls runs a frieze of remarkable Navaho paintings done by a brave who was certainly the worse for numerous hookers of redeye and which was purchased on a Western honeymoon. A most amusing spot in which to work. It suits its owner to a T.

Struggles for individuality may take perseverance. My own most successful kitchen, which combined canary-yellow walls and Kelly-green woodwork with chinese-orange shelf and cupboard linings, was only achieved by the constant browbeating of a country painter. Two days it was that the house resounded to the irritated slap of his brush, accompanied by mutterings of "Never seed sech colors!" "This ain't fittin' fer a kitchen!" and the constantly repeated "She won't like it when I done it." *She* did, though, and so did her friends and even the "artist" rather shamefacedly admitted that "it weren't too bad."

Once satisfied with your surroundings, wallow in a little deserved selfishness and plan your own personal decoration by means of an ample supply of becoming aprons. The chances are you'll be seen in them much more often than in that expensive formal gown that took hours of choosing, so put care into the selection. If you're the type, ruffle away to your heart's content and leave the tailored models to your tweedy sister. Be sure the donning won't disarrange a newly brushed topnot, that they cover you adequately, and that they take to soap and water like a dish towel. In fact, a brightly printed dish towel makes a very good apron. Sew a loop of tape on one end about 8 inches apart and long enough to slip easily over your head, tack an 18-inch piece of tape on each long side at your waistline, slip it on, tie the strings, *et voilà du chic, madame!* Not to mention effective protection against the biggest splash.

Its designer's former claim to fame, the invention of colored cocktail toothpicks, isn't half so useful as the practical apron pattern on this book's end papers. It only takes a yard of material and, made in a flowered print, and edged with eyelet embroidery will serve the gayest buffet supper, while its workmanlike heavy cotton twin hangs in the kitchen to help with the cleaning-up. Sew the leftover scraps into pot-holders and fasten them to the ends of a yard-long piece of tape, and with this handy contrivance slung around your neck while cooking, never again will you have to cast a wild look around for aid in picking up a hot dish.

A small blackboard and its chalk may not be a decoration, but it's a fine useful thing on the kitchen wall. While mine frequently carries such messages as "Where did you put the bottle opener, you bum?" amidst reminders of necessary tomatoes or eggs, it saves many a phone call or trip to the store for otherwise forgotten articles.

Cookbooks, with their bright-colored jackets *are* decorative. Please don't hide them away in the back of a dark pantry drawer, but flaunt your business library proudly on open shelves. Everyone has one tried and true dog-eared book of instruction which is as useful for looking up standard recipes as a dictionary for looking up words. Bring it out boldly, and since source books conveniently at hand make for much more varied and easier menus, let it have for companions not only those well-bound volumes containing the dishes you've always "meant to try," but also the humbler paper pamphlets of recipes that so many food and domestic-appliance companies send out at the drop of a coupon. Biased these must be—hence their publication—but they often hide nuggets of real value. When a recipe has proved successful, write the name and page number on the flyleaf of its book or underline it in the index.

Hark, now, to the frenzied moaning of bibliophiles at that last suggestion! Will it be of any use to point out that cookbooks are printed to be consulted and not cherished behind glass doors! All right, perhaps it is better to make an orderly file of the same information like a truly tidy pachyderm, but to me and to many others it's enough effort to be a good cook.

And if this volume remains in your kitchen to become well thumbed, worn and even spotted, I shall feel happier and much more successful than if years from now it turns up in pristine condition in a locked bookcase as a collector's item.

Selected Recipes

by ELIZABETH GILBERT

Gentle Reader, one more thing: While I believe that a good part of this cookbook's charm is in my great-grandmother's voice—that wonderful, wandering, narrative way in which she tells the story of each recipe—I also recognize that telling a recipe is not quite the same thing as simply noting it, and sometimes her recipes can be tricky to weed through, especially if you're in a hurry. For that reason, I offer up these top ten favorite family recipes—simply noted—drawn from the book and transcribed very clearly for easier reproduction. It wasn't easy to choose ten favorites from such a rich body of work, but these are the foods I grew up eating, before I even knew I was eating out of my great-grandmother's masterpiece. The Chutney is particularly lovely, and was a constant presence on our family table throughout my entire youth. The Quick Tea Cookies are a godsend for last-minute guests. The Pot Roast tastes like an intimate homecoming. The Kidney Stew is just a weird family predilection: I won't even try to defend it here, other than to say, This Is Who We Are. And as for the Fruitcake: Good Luck. You'll see that Gima didn't leave out a single step—so don't you go easy on yourself, either. This is a go-big-or-go-home recipe. If you're gonna do it, do it all the way. Don't falter! If you need fruit-cake fortitude, just imagine my terrific great-grandmother standing over your shoulder—a cocktail in one hand, a cigarette in the other—laughing and encouraging you and just generally having a ball.

Sour Milk Muffins

From page 145. Makes 12 regular-sized muffins, or 24 minis.

- 1 egg, yolk and white separated
- 1 cup sour milk
- 1 cup flour
- ½ tsp baking soda

- 1 tsp sugar
- 1 tsp salt
- 1 tbsp oil or melted butter, plus more for greasing the tins

1. Preheat the oven to 400° and grease the muffin tins.
2. Beat the egg yolk, and add the sour milk. Together, sift the flour, baking soda, sugar, and salt. Stir this into the egg yolk/milk mixture.
3. Beat the egg white to a soft peak, and gently fold that into the mixture, along with the oil or melted butter. *Do not* add the oil/butter directly to the egg white, as this will cause your whites to deflate immediately.
4. Pour into greased muffin tins and bake at 400° for 10 minutes for small muffins, or 15 minutes for standard muffins.

LIZ'S NOTES

- How to make sour milk: either leave 1 cup of milk out overnight to sour, or add 1 tbsp of white vinegar or lemon juice to slightly less than 1 cup of milk—so that the final measure is 1 cup of liquid—mix together and let stand for about 10 minutes to thicken.
- The muffins will have very little color on top when finished—do not be alarmed!

YOUR NOTES

Kidney Stew

From page 190. Makes 2–4 servings.

- 1 large or 2 small beef kidneys
- 1 onion, peeled and chopped
- 1 stalk of celery, chopped
- 1 sprig of parsley, chopped
- 3 tbsp butter
- 2 tbsp flour

- 2 eggs
- 1 tsp Worcestershire sauce
- 1 tbsp sherry
- salt, black pepper, and cayenne pepper to taste
- cornstarch, as needed

1. Cover the kidney with water in a pot, and simmer for 15 minutes over medium heat. Scum and fat will cloud the water. Wash off the kidney, so you're left with a smaller, paler kidney.
2. Place the kidney in a slow cooker or dutch oven, along with the onion, celery, and parsley. Cover it all with water, and bring it to a simmer. Let it cook 6–8 hours.
3. Take it off the heat, and add a pinch of salt. Once reasonably cool, take the kidney out, and cut it into bite-sized pieces, discarding the center. Strain the fat from the water, and save the water in a separate bowl.
4. Hard-boil the eggs while you're doing step 5.
5. In a saucepan, melt the butter, and slowly add in the flour, mixing as you go. Once that bubbles, slowly add in 3 cups of the kidney water. Simmer for 10 minutes.
6. Chop the hard-boiled eggs, and add them with the chopped kidneys to your gravy/broth. Simmer for another 10 minutes. If it's not thick enough, add cornstarch. Add the Worcestershire and sherry, and then season to taste with salt, black pepper, and cayenne pepper.

LIZ'S NOTES

- A slow cooker or dutch oven is ideal for this recipe.

YOUR NOTES

Fruitcake

From page 114. Fills 8 standard loaf pans.

- 3 lbs currants
- 1½ lbs raisins with seeds
- 1½ lbs raisins without seeds
- 1 lb dates, cut into small pieces
- 1 lb candied citron
- ¼ lb candied lemon peel
- ¼ lb candied orange peel
- ½ lb candied cherries (halve each cherry)
- ½ cup rum
- 1 lb butter
- 1 lb light brown sugar

- 12 eggs
- ¾ cup molasses
- ½ cup brandy or rye whiskey
- 4 cups flour
- 1 tbsp cinnamon
- 1 tbsp nutmeg
- 1 tbsp mace
- ½ tsp ground cloves
- ½ tsp allspice
- 8 tbsps rum, sherry, whiskey, or brandy
- oil or lard, for greasing pans

1. Mix the fruits and peels together and sprinkle the rum over them.
2. Using an electric mixer, cream the butter with the light brown sugar. Beat all 12 eggs until they're light, and add to the butter and sugar, along with the molasses and brandy or rye whiskey, and beat again. Sift into this the flour, cinnamon, nutmeg, mace, cloves, and allspice. Beat again. Pour the batter over the fruits and peels, and mix thoroughly until every piece is coated.
3. Grease the chosen pans or casseroles with oil or lard. Line the bottoms and sides with parchment paper and grease that, too.

4. Pat the completed cake batter gently into its pans up to the three-quarter mark. Bake smaller cakes for 3½ hours and the large bread-pan size for 4 hours—both in a 275° oven that has a pan filled with water on the bottom. Turn the cakes out of the pans and remove the paper when hot. Cool and dribble 1 tablespoon of liquor (rum, sherry, whiskey, or brandy) over each cake.

5. Stack the cakes for at least 2 months in a covered crock or a tin breadbox that has been lined with wax paper, turning them over every 2 weeks or so and dribbling more liquor on top.

6. Before eating or giving away, decorate the cakes with leaves and berries of sliced citron and candied cherries, gluing them on with a syrup of ½ cup sugar and ¼ cup of water that has been boiled until a few drops become brittle when dropped in ice water. Wrap each cake carefully in double layers of waxed paper or cellophane before tying up in holiday tissue.

LIZ'S NOTES

- Your cakes may be ready in 3 hours. You can tell it's done when no crumbs stick to a toothpick or knife that you prod the cake with, and the cake appears to pull away from the sides of the pan.

YOUR NOTES

_____

_____

_____

Chicken Livers with Red Wine

From page 52. Makes 8 servings.

- 1 tbsp chopped onion or chives
- 1 tsp parsley, chopped
- ½ lb mushrooms, sliced
- 3 tbsp butter
- 1 lb chicken livers
- 3 tbsp flour

- 1 tsp salt
- A little pepper
- 1 cup dry red wine
- 2 cup bouillon, consommé, or chicken broth

1. Sauté the onion/chives, parsley, and mushrooms in the butter until the onion/chives are soft.
2. Dust the chicken livers with flour, salt, and pepper. Add them to the pan. Let them cook for 5 minutes. Add the red wine and bouillon/consommé/broth. Cook 10 minutes until thickened. Serve in a ring of cooked rice, and with fried eggplant.

LIZ'S NOTES

- 4 cups of cooked rice are the ideal quantity for this recipe.

YOUR NOTES

Pot Roast

From page 48. Makes 8 servings.

- 1 piece of 4- or 5-lb top round beef
- 1 pint red wine (claret or Burgundy)
- 2 onions, sliced
- 1 garlic clove, crushed
- ½ cup celery, finely chopped
- 1 pinch of thyme
- 1 bay leaf (if you like it)
- 1 tsp flour

- 4 oz suet, salt pork, or other fat, chopped
- 4 tomatoes, peeled
- 2 or more onions, peeled
- 2 or more whole carrots, peeled
- 3–4 turnips, peeled
- 2 packages of broad noodles
- 1 tsp salt (and more for step 4)
- A dash of pepper
- ½ cup sour cream
- Flour or cornstarch, as needed

1. Put the meat into a shallow bowl, pour the wine over, and add the onions, garlic, celery, a pinch of thyme, and a bay leaf if you like the taste. Let it soak for 24 hours at least, turning the meat every 8 hours or so. When you are ready to cook, drain the meat thoroughly, reserving the wine (sans bay leaf), and mop it as dry as possible, using a paper towel lightly.

2. Dust the meat with flour. Now fry the suet or salt pork in a heavy-bottomed pot. Put in the beef and brown it thoroughly on all sides, pour in the wine marinade, add the tomatoes, and let it simmer, tightly covered, for 1 hour.

3. Add the onions and carrots, as well as the turnips, salt, and pepper.

Simmer for about another hour, or until the vegetables are done.

4. In the meantime, have ready 2 packages of broad noodles that have been boiled in plenty of salted water. Drain them and keep them hot in a colander over boiling water.

5. Put your roast on a large hot platter, and thicken the gravy with sour cream while bringing the juice to a low boil. Add a little cornstarch or flour mixed with cold water if it's not thick enough. Place the vegetables around the roast, then decorate the edge of the dish with hot boiled noodles, each mound of which has a bit of butter on top. Serve the gravy separately.

LIZ'S NOTES

- The meat might take longer than an hour. It's cooked when it yields easily to a fork. Don't be alarmed if it takes 3 hours.
- In place of suet, try a solid and firm beef fat (kidney fat is good for this, and may come free if you're making Kidney Stew).
- Gima recommends 2 peeled onions and 2 peeled carrots per person. As many as you can fit into the pot will work, too.
- Mixing the flour or cornstarch with the sour cream before adding it to the gravy will keep it from curdling.

YOUR NOTES

Chutney

From page 130. Makes about 3 pints.

- 4 cups apples (Granny Smith or similarly tart), sliced
- 6 cups green (not yet ripe) tomatoes, sliced
- 2 cups onion, chopped
- 1 clove garlic, minced
- 1 cup raisins
- 1 tbsp candied ginger, minced

- 1 cup vinegar
- 4 cups brown sugar
- 3 tsp salt
- 1 tsp mustard seed
- 1 tsp cinnamon
- ½ tsp ground cloves
- ⅛ tsp cayenne pepper

1. Put everything in a pot in the order above.
2. Bring to a simmer, while stirring everything together. Simmer for 2 hours, or until the fruit breaks down and the liquid thickens to a syrupy consistency. Make sure to stir more frequently towards the end, to avoid burning the bottom.
3. Seal in sterilized jars.

LIZ'S NOTES

- It's roughly 1 apple or tomato per cup, but varies depending on the size of the fruit.
- Gima's recipe says it's 6 pints, but as tested, it's about half that.

YOUR NOTES

P.O.M. Pickles

From page 131. Makes about 6–8 quarts.

- 2 quarts green (not yet ripe) tomatoes, chopped
- 1 quart white onions, peeled and chopped
- 1 bunch celery, chopped
- 4 bell peppers (2 green, 2 red), seeded and chopped
- 2 cucumbers, peeled and chopped
- 1 pint sweet pickles
- 1 quart sour (or dill) pickles
- 1 large or 2 small heads of cauliflower
- ½ cup salt

For the paste in step 4
- vinegar
- dry mustard
- turmeric
- brown sugar
- flour
- cayenne pepper

For the bundle in step 5
- 2 tbsp whole allspice
- 1 tbsp whole cloves
- 1 tbsp cinnamon
- 2 tbsp mustard seed

1. Chop the sweet and sour pickles. Pull off bits of the cauliflower, and chop the stems. Put everything in the biggest pot you have. Add the salt, and cover everything with water. Let it stand overnight.
2. Bring the vegetable mix to a boil, then drain the water, returning the vegetables to the pot.
3. Cover with vinegar, making sure to measure how much you're pouring.
4. For every 3 pints of vinegar used in step 3, mix proportionally:
   6 tbsp dry mustard
   1 tbsp turmeric

3 cups brown sugar

½ cup flour

⅛ tsp cayenne pepper

Add vinegar to this mix in small amounts, stirring as you do, until it's a thick paste. Mix this in with the vegetables.

5. Using cheesecloth and twine, bundle up the allspice, cloves, cinnamon, and mustard seed. Add it to the pot. Simmer for 15 minutes, stirring as it heats.

6. Remove the cheesecloth packet, turn off the heat, and jar the pickle mix. Let the sealed jars sit for at least 2 weeks before eating.

LIZ'S NOTES

- 6–8 quarts is *a lot* of food. If you do not have a very large pot, you'll have to cut the recipe down by half, or more.
- As Gima notes, you can add just about any vegetable to this.

YOUR NOTES

Oyster Bisque

From page 42. Makes 4 servings.

- 2 or 3 oysters, juice reserved
- 2 tbsp butter
- 2 tbsp flour
- 2 cups milk
- 1 tsp salt
- ⅛ tsp black pepper

1. Add 2 or 3 chopped oysters to 1 pint of their strained juice and bring to a boil.
2. Make white sauce: In a saucepan, melt the butter over a medium flame and stir in the flour. When it starts to bubble take the pan from the fire and slowly stir 1 cup of milk, letting the flour absorb the liquid. Put the pan back over the heat and just as slowly add 1 cup more of milk, never ceasing the constant stirring.
3. Add the salt and black pepper, and keep it over a lower heat for at least 10 minutes longer, stirring occasionally. If you must neglect it after the last milk goes in, put the sauce into the top of a double boiler to finish cooking over hot water.
4. Mix the steaming oysters and juice into the white sauce, and serve.

LIZ'S NOTES

- If your oysters do not supply you the pint of liquid, bottled clam or oyster juice works, too.
- Use a heavy-bottomed saucepan and a whisk for the white sauce.

YOUR NOTES

Celery au Gratin

From page 91. Makes 4–6 servings.

- 2 cups celery stalks, cut crosswise in 1-inch lengths
- 2½ cups white sauce, as described in the Oyster Bisque
- ½ cup bread crumbs

- ½ cup grated cheese (such as Gruyère or Parmigiano-Reggiano)
- 4 tbsp butter
- salt

1. Boil the celery in salted water until tender. Drain, and mix with white sauce and grated cheese.
2. Butter a dish with half of the butter. Add the celery/sauce/cheese mixture, cover it with bread crumbs, and dot it with the other half the butter. Bake at 400° for 20 minutes or until the crumbs are brown.

LIZ'S NOTES

- Gima does not specify what type of "grated cheese" to use, but Gruyère yields a particularly delicious gratin.
- Keep an eye on your bread crumbs to make sure they don't burn. If they start to look too brown too early, cover the whole thing with foil and keep cooking.

YOUR NOTES

Quick Tea Cookies

From page 121. Makes 8–12 small cookies.

- 2 tbsp brown sugar (and a few more pinches for step 2)
- 2 tbsp butter, softened
- 1 egg, well-beaten
- ½ cup flour, sifted

- 1 pinch of salt
- 1 pinch cinnamon
- 2 pinches of nutmeg
- 1 tsp caraway seeds (optional)

1. Cream the brown sugar and butter. Add the egg, sifted flour, salt, cinnamon, and nutmeg; beat well.

   1a. This is when Gima says you can add 1 tsp of caraway seeds to the batter "if you like the old-fashioned flavor."

2. Drop by small flattened spoonfuls, well apart, on a greased cookie (or "cooky"!) sheet. Put a pinch of brown sugar on the top of each cookie and bake 8 minutes in a 425° oven.

   2a. You can also add a half-walnut or a sliced, blanched almond on top of each cookie before baking.

LIZ'S NOTES

- These aren't what you'd typically think of as cookies today. They're more like tiny cakes, best enjoyed immediately after they're baked.

YOUR NOTES

Index

About ScholarMatch

ScholarMatch's mission is to connect under-resourced students with donors and make college accessible. Launched in 2010 by 826 National, ScholarMatch crowdsources funds to fill the gap in college scholarships for high-achieving San Francisco Bay Area students with significant financial need. We also provide college-success programming and workshops in our office in San Francisco.

More than 80 percent of ScholarMatch students are the first in their families to go to college, and over 50 percent live in families with annual incomes of less than $25,000 a year. ScholarMatch students are dedicated, committed, and have overcome harrowing challenges, and yet have maintained their determination to seek a better future though college.

By buying this book, you've already donated to ScholarMatch.
Thank you!

But here's how you can help even more:

- Any donation size helps! The ScholarMatch students who have reached their scholarship goal did so through the generosity of multiple donors.
- Donate as a group! Get your friends, your book group, or your company to support a ScholarMatch student.
- An average of $5,000 will fund one year of college for a ScholarMatch student.
- A donation of $10,000 will fund the scholarship goals of at least two or more students.

With commitments from donors, we can help ensure that young people receive the education they need to help them succeed in a challenging economic landscape. By purchasing this book, you are joining us in our work. And by donating, you are, in a very direct way, sending an underserved student to college.

Thank you.
ScholarMatch

www.scholarmatch.org

About 826 National

Founded in 2002, 826 National is a nationwide network of nonprofit writing and tutoring centers that provides students, ages 6–18, with opportunities to explore their creativity and improve their writing skills. From after-school homework help to innovative writing workshops and in-schools publishing projects, 826 programs are offered for free and are rooted in the understanding that great leaps in learning can happen with one-on-one attention, and that strong writing skills are fundamental to future success. During the 2010–2011 school year, 826 centers—located in San Francisco, New York, Ann Arbor, Boston, Chicago, Los Angeles, Seattle, and Washington, DC—served nearly 30,000 students from under-resourced communities and schools. To learn more about 826 National's work, or to volunteer or donate, please visit:

www.826national.org

Other McSweeney's Publications

McSweeney's is a small, independent publishing company based in San Francisco. In addition to our namesake Quarterly of award-winning short fiction and design, we also publish children's books, art books, comics, and a wide array of fiction and nonfiction. Below are a handful of things you might be interested in. For more information, visit us at store.mcsweeneys.net, or seek out and support your local independent bookstore.

The Latke Who Couldn't Stop Screaming
by Lemony Snicket

Latkes are potato pancakes served at Hanukah. Lemony Snicket is an alleged children's author. For the first time in literary history, these two elements are combined in one book. People who are interested in either or both of these things will find this book so enjoyable it will feel as if Hanukah is being celebrated for several years, rather than eight nights. People who are interested in neither of these things will get what they deserve.

The Latke Who Couldn't Stop Screaming is hardcover, foil-stamped, and full of colorful illustrations, well-suited for giving, receiving, or clutching selfishly in trembling hands.

Lucky Peach

Lucky Peach is a quarterly journal of food writing, edited by award-winning chef David Chang, writer Peter Meehan, and longtime McSweeney's editor

Chris Ying. It is a mélange of travelogue, essays, art, photography, rants, and recipes in a full-color, meticulously designed format. Averaging 176 pages of nearly ad-free content, our aim is to produce a publication that appeals to diehard foodies as well as fans of good writing and art in general.

"[*Lucky Peach*] breaks many of the conventions not only of food journalism, but of magazine journalism in general.... A glorious, improbable artifact, [and a] hit among the food-obsessed.... A reminder of print's true wingspan."
—David Carr, *The New York Times*

Mission Street Food
by Anthony Myint and Karen Leibovitz

ONE OF "THE BEST COOKBOOKS FOR HOLIDAY GIFTS" BY THE *LA TIMES*

A 2011 NEW YORK TIMES NOTABLE COOKBOOK

ONE OF BON APPETIT'S BEST COOKBOOKS OF 2011

Mission Street Food is a restaurant. But it's also a charitable organization, a taco truck, a burger stand, and a clubhouse for inventive cooks tucked inside an unassuming Chinese take-out place. In all its various incarnations, it upends traditional restaurant conventions, in search of moral and culinary satisfaction.

Like Mission Street Food itself, this book is more than one thing: it's a cookbook featuring step-by-step photography and sly commentary, but it's also the memoir of a madcap project that redefined the authors' marriage and a city's food scene. Along with stories and recipes, you'll find an idealistic business plan, a cheeky manifesto, and thoughtful essays on issues ranging from food pantries to fried chicken. Plus, a comic.

"An amazing story. An amazing institution." —Anthony Bourdain

About the Authors

ELIZABETH GILBERT is the bestselling author of numerous books, including *Eat, Pray, Love*, now a major motion picture. In 2008, *Time* magazine named Elizabeth as one of the 100 most influential people in the world.

MARGARET YARDLEY POTTER's book is culled from a lifetime of cooking and entertaining in her home, from the 1920s through World War II. In addition to being a cooking columnist for the *Wilmington Star*, she also painted, sold dresses, assisted in the birth of four grandchildren, and took up swing piano.